CW00584865

BOB'S JOURNEY AFTER DEATH

ANNIE NEE ELLIS

CHAPTER ONE

Bob slowly opened the large door leading to his garage and gazed admiringly at his brand new motorbike. The bright red metal frame sparkled in the sunlight and the powerful engine stood out as a symbol of freedom.

He felt excited and couldn't wait to take it out on to the open roads.

But he paused for a moment as if questioning himself. Then said out loud, ' Sod them all, let's go and burn some rubber and show you off to my mates.'

He knew that he shouldn't be driving as he had been banned, but he didn't care. He jumped on his bike and roared off down the road loving the cool breeze on his face and the sun on his back, unaware of what lay ahead.

He was contemplating his life so far, it seemed to have gone by so quickly. He had married a lovely girl and they had two boys, both now grown up and married. He was in his late forties still working and had a steady job in retail.

But when the boys had grown up and left home, his wife had divorced him.

She complained that he was too controlling, wanting to know where she was and what she was doing at all times. Now that the boys had left home, she wanted more freedom to pursue her own hobbies and spend more time with her friends.

Discussions became heated as she became more assertive. How dare she stand up to him like that, he thought. She had never complained much before. Though he didn't like to admit it, he had expected everyone to jump to his commands and had kept his family on a tight leash.

He lived alone now, though did have a couple of mates he often met up with at the local pub. But his children didn't contact him very often, they had been glad to leave home and enjoy the freedom of being in control of their own lives.

Some months ago Bob had noticed that he seemed to be getting very forgetful.
It was small things at first, such as often losing his keys, or forgetting where he had put his shoes. But more worryingly, he found that recently he couldn't remember people's names, even friends he had known for years.

He even forgot his own birthday when the bank had asked for his date of birth for security reasons.

He was very embarrassed and began to think that something may be wrong, his memory was awful.

After he had burnt a few meals by forgetting that the oven was on, he decided to mention it to the doctor. A thorough examination was conducted and the doctor had then referred him to hospital for further tests.

The consultant told him that unfortunately he had early signs of dementia and although a new drug may slow the progress, he would eventually get worse. Bob didn't believe them at first, he thought dementia was an old person's disease and he certainly didn't feel old yet, he was only middle aged.

The doctors eventually got through to him, after he was shown the test results and scans. He hated the thought of losing control and being looked after by others, it was his worst nightmare.

He knew that if he told his ex wife, she would happily have him back and look after him. But being put into that position of being cared for, was too much for Bob who was used to being in control. He couldn't stand the thought of becoming subservient and helpless, so for now he decided to ignore it altogether.

He promised to attend the next appointment with someone who could help with the planning of his future needs, but he actually had no intention of telling his mates or anybody else.

So after getting over the shock, he had decided to go and buy a new motorbike. His reasoning was that he

may as well enjoy what normal life he had left, a last fling at freedom whilst he could.
Of course he had been told not to drive, but who were *they,* telling *him,* Bob what to do.
He planned to visit every pub in the county, have a pint with his mates and enjoy himself.

He opened the throttle, loving the speed and roar of the engine and raced up the straight narrow road. Up ahead on the other side of the road, a car pulled out to overtake another and was heading straight for him.

Oh God ! The driver hadn't seen him. Bob couldn't think what to do, he shouted,

'OH CRAP' and the car ploughed straight into him.

There was mayhem on the road, bits of bike and car strewn everywhere.
Cars stopped, people got out looking shocked. For a minute Bob couldn't think what was going on.
He seemed to be hovering above the scene watching everything from above, as though he was watching a movie.

Soon he noticed that one of his mates, Ron, had joined him.
Bob talked about the carnage below. 'what a bloody mess, look at that poor bugger lying in the road, doesn't look good does it.'
Bob was about to say something else, when he suddenly remembered that Ron had actually died a

couple of years ago.
He had gone to his funeral, bought flowers, had a toast to him with his mates to see him off and yet here he was standing next to him, he felt confused.

He couldn't think what to say at first, but he felt overjoyed to see his old mate.
'It's great to see you Ron, but am I dreaming? you died two years ago.'
Ron laughed, 'This is no dream, it's very real, you know that you died in that crash don't you. That is your new bike isn't it and your body lying there. That car certainly did a lot of damage, nobody could have survived that crash.'

Bob looked very carefully at all the mayhem below and suddenly realised it was true. That was definitely his bike, and although he looked a mess because he had been thrown into a muddy puddle, it was definitely him.

He wondered what was happening, everything around him felt very real. In fact it felt as if his mind had expanded somehow and he could tell what individual people were thinking. He could tell that one woman who was standing next to her car, was worried because she had to pick her daughter up from school.

'Don't worry Ron said, you will feel a bit disorientated because you passed so quickly.

I felt the same at first when I died, especially when I saw my mother who had died years before.

She had come to meet me, I couldn't believe it at first, it was so lovely to see her though. Everything will become clear to you soon, just relax. You will love it here Bob, I have so much to tell you.'

Bob saw somebody else coming over to join them, he recognised him at once though not from his life on earth.
It was Alistair who was always there for him, a friend and mentor, he was Bob's spiritual guide. He looked young, about twenty five, but Bob felt that he was much older.
Although he was wearing ordinary clothes, jeans and a shirt, there was a kind of aura surrounding him. Bob felt calm and relaxed in his presence.

Bob was so happy to see him. 'I can't believe this, seeing you both and I feel better than I have done for years, but what can we do about that mess below and my brand new motorbike, that's going to take some work.'

'We can't do anything here, Alistair said, you don't belong here now. When you are a bit more settled, you can come back and see how your mates are doing, they usually can't see you of course but they can often sense your presence.'

Ron said that he had to leave but would catch up later and Alistair offered to take Bob home. 'There are friends waiting to see you, they are so excited, come on.'

The road was becoming more chaotic with traffic, people and ambulances everywhere, so Bob was glad to leave. They left the scene below and Bob found himself walking effortlessly along with Alistair, following a tree lined path toward a bright light in the distance.

He still felt a bit confused, but at the same time knew that all was well.
He realised that he had died, but didn't even feel anxious or worried, everywhere felt calm and relaxed, and being with Alistair was wonderful.
They chatted as they walked along.
'You will remember everything soon, even your friends here,' Alistair said.

They stopped at a building that looked like a beautiful town hall with many pillars all along the front. They reminded Bob of the inside of a pearl shell when he looked at them, sort of luminescent, and the building seemed to have a certain glow surrounding it.

'This is one of the places we have that will cleanse and adjust your energy. All the fears and anxiety that you have felt in your life will be integrated into your soul experience and then left behind. You have lived in fear for some time so you will find this amazing.'

Bob walked in through a very ornate archway and was immediately surrounded by light rays of many colours and hues.

It seemed to have a hypnotic power that was irresistible and Bob began to feel a wonderful change happening within him. He felt calm and at peace, any sadness, anxiety and worry just seemed to melt away, and he felt infused with a loving energy.

He also began to remember who he really was and where he belonged, as though he had come home.
As they came out of the building Bob felt so happy, he saw other souls as they walked along, he knew that each person was a soul because they were surrounded with an energy field of different coloured light.

They waved to him and Bob felt as though he belonged, as though he was part of them all, not as on earth where you feel separate from everybody else.

He had usually been aloof and could be quite rude to others, but now he felt excited and happy as they walked through a beautiful tree lined Avenue.

'I hope everyone has this wonderful experience when they die,' said Bob.

'Oh yes, most people are met by their loved ones who come to greet them, it makes the transition easier and enjoyable. Everybody also has their own spirit guide who would always be there to greet them.

Occasionally we even take a favourite pet of theirs, a dog or cat for example, just to make it easier for them. They will soon find they have plenty of friends over here.'

'Really, are there dogs and cats here too,' asked Bob.

'Of course, all animals and birds and insects have their own realm that they inhabit, but they can choose to stay with us if we want, as we form very close bonds with our animal friends. There are also horses and the odd cow,' laughed Alistair.

'Well, who would have thought, I suppose angels with wings playing harps are a bit of a myth then.' 'Yes they are, but if you believe you will be met by angels when you die, then that is what will be manifested for your immediate experience to help you feel at ease until you are properly integrated here.'

'What about ghosts, Bob asked, are they real.' 'Yes, said Alistair, occasionally someone may not want to leave where they are after death.
Perhaps they have money or jewellery or other objects of importance hidden away, and can't bear to leave them behind, they can feel very angry when strange people move into their home.

Also, time has no meaning after death, one year or a hundred years will seem to be the same. It can be quite a challenge to entice them away, though eventually they do trust us and come with us.
I actually work with earthbound souls, it's something that I love to do.

Sometimes though, what you may think are ghosts,

are actually a sort of replay of past events. Nothing that happens is ever lost, the energy is indestructible and sometimes you can tune into a past event. This usually happens where the energy is of a higher vibration.

There are energy points on the earth sometimes where ley lines cross and under the right atmospheric conditions you may for instance, see Roman soldiers marching across a road. These are not usually souls that are still hanging around on earth, but a sort of replay of past events in the atmosphere, especially in places where intense emotions have been involved, such as a battle.

Also many of us often spend time on earth with our loved ones, especially at first when they are feeling sad. So of course, we are ghosts, and though most cannot see us, they can usually sense our presence.

To answer your original question though, everybody is unique and it depends on your beliefs before death.

Many of us don't give it much thought until we are actually facing death, but then there is not that much knowledge regarding what happens afterwards.

Some cultures commonly think that you will be judged by angels or God before they will let you enter through some pearly gates, or you will go to hell where a devil will torment you if you have misbehaved.

All man-made stories of course, it was not that long

ago people believed children would not enter heaven if they had not been baptised.'

Bob had witnessed this himself. He told Alistair that when he had decided that his first child would not be christened, his mother in law was most upset. So much so, that he had to give in eventually.

`Religion is not helpful if it is based on fear,' said Alistair. He began to discuss how, when the end of your life was near, it would be better to concentrate your thoughts on those loved ones who had already died, and look forward to meeting them, when Bob suddenly realised, they were not talking in the normal sense with their mouths, but seemed to be directly communicating with each other.

Bob could hear his thoughts quite clearly. 'Aaah yes, said Alistair, we speak telepathically here, as we are no longer in a human body with limited senses.

You send out a thought and we can pick it up and respond, similar to speech in a way because you have to think about what you are going to say first before you speak, so we are bypassing the speech part.

It's very efficient don't you think, though we can't pick up your private thoughts, only what you want to say in a general conversation.

Bob liked this way of communicating, it felt very

natural and easy. He also noticed there seemed to be no effort in walking, though usually his right knee would be hurting by now after a fall had damaged it when he was playing football with his mates.

Soon they arrived at a beautiful courtyard, with brightly coloured patterned tiles on the floor.

There was a very large shiny black rock in the middle where water came bubbling up and cascaded all over it sending rainbows in all directions.

The surrounding buildings were lovely, some had archways and others had nice green shutters. A few had a small balcony where flowering plants cascaded down from them, they were very ornate. Most were a lovely light cream colour and had a mother of pearl luminescence look.

There were wonderful flowers everywhere, which were the most amazing colours, some of which Bob had never seen before.

He stood next to a plant which had huge yellow and orange flowers all over it, and the scent was just intoxicating. As he looked at the flowers, he could feel their energy, and on their level as if part of them.
It was a very calming and beautiful place to be.

As they entered the courtyard, several young people came over to greet Bob, they were so happy to see him. Bob immediately recognised them as his closest friends, where they were always together, playing together, experiencing new things and growing together.

'I'll leave for a while and let you celebrate and catch up'. said Alistair. He wasn't part of their group, he was an older, wiser soul who was a guide and mentor to Bob and the others. They all loved him.

Bob was so happy to be back with his friends, they chatted and laughed and Bob felt as though he hadn't been away for long.

He knew them all very well, these were his soulmates, they were a small group of six like minded and similar souls. They were an outgoing bunch who enjoyed exploring and travelling.

Bob saw that there were many other groups of souls, some of whom interacted with his. They were in groups together because of their similarities.
So you would have soul groups who were all adventurous types, or maybe flamboyant, or some groups were quiet and thoughtful.
But being similar meant that they understood each other and had similar experiences together and grew together.

One of his friends called Eliza, took him on a tour around, she told him that there had been some changes since he was last there.
The courtyard was part of a bigger area similar to a plaza, here were the most beautiful fountains with white stone that had a luminescence from the light that was all around.

It wasn't sunlight as there was no actual sun, but a form of energy that bathed everything in a nice ambient light.

The water that cascaded from the fountains was magical, you could feel the lively energy and immerse yourself in it. The colours everywhere were vibrant with many more different shades and hues of colour. The buildings around the plaza were much larger, each one different but a lovely cream colour and all were beautifully designed, Bob couldn't get over how beautiful it was, he thought it was amazing.

Eliza took Bob back to the courtyard and showed him a pretty stone coloured building that had three windows, one with a balcony. It had gorgeous blue scented flowers climbing all over it. It reminded Bob of a pretty village he had visited once on a mediterranean island.

'Go on in, she said, this is your house, your home.'
Bob walked inside and immediately loved it, it was bright and airy and even had chairs and a table and curtains at the windows.
'This is just the type of house I dreamed of having on earth, he said, I would even have chosen that Moroccan pattern for the rugs on the floor.'

'Everything here is made very much the same so that it feels familiar and makes you happy.

All the things that you have wished for in life, are all there in an energy form, so this home is what you imagined and it was created for you.'

They sat at the table, and as Bob thought it would be nice to have a cup of coffee, he suddenly noticed his own coffee pot and two cups on the table.

Eliza laughed, 'you must have been thinking about coffee. We don't need to eat or drink here, but most people feel happier with their old familiar routine for a while, but you soon realise that these things aren't necessary.

I couldn't do without my cup of tea at first as it had been such an important part of my life.

When I walked into my house and saw my old teapot on the table, I felt really happy, but these small things help you to settle in because after all you are still the same person and it would be overwhelming if you found yourself in a completely different environment.

Our vibrational energy is very high here, so that you can manifest anything you want really easily. You can have things that were important to you while you were on earth, such as coffee or cakes or even golf clubs, at least while you think you need them.'

'So, could I have a hot curry or a pizza?' asked Bob.
'Yes but don't expect your mouth to burn or your face to sweat.' laughed Eliza.

Bob felt pleased that he could get instant takeaways, he thought about what else he would like.
'Can I go sailing in a boat on a lake?' he asked. 'Oh yes, others do that too, there is so much to do, you will

never feel bored.'

Bob loved his new home though he noticed there were one or two things missing.

Eliza explained, 'we don't need bedrooms, because we no longer need to sleep, though we do rest sometimes, and because we don't need food or water to sustain us anymore, a kitchen with a cooker and fridge would be pretty useless.'

Bob was pleased, he hated cooking. 'Come on, she said, I want to show you my place.'
They went out into the square and walked (though it felt very effortless) up a tree lined lane off the plaza. There arrived at a row of pretty cottages at the end of the lane and Eliza went into the first one.

'This is my home, I always dreamed of having a house like this when I was on earth.'
They went inside, it was very cosy with two large armchairs, a table and some pretty curtains at the window. Then Bob noticed a black cat with white paws lying on the window sill.

'Oh, that's a surprise to see a cat lying there.' said Bob. Eliza explained, 'he was my best friend on earth, I had him as a kitten and he slept on my bed every night and kept me company.

My sister had died so I often felt lonely and he was such a comfort. He will stay as long as I want him to and is very happy to be here with me.'

As Bob looked at the cat, he distinctly heard him

say 'Nice to meet you Bob.' He was rather taken aback by this and Eliza laughed.

'Oh it's alright, we all communicate through telepathy here and so can also understand what animals are saying to us.'

'I was as surprised as you when I first came here and found my beloved cat in the house, and that we could talk to each other. I learnt that all animals and other creatures are far more aware than we think they are.

When you have acclimatised to this environment it will feel much more natural, in fact, *here,* is your natural state of being.

Earth is just a short term place we inhabit in order to experience something. You have to drag your body around everywhere you go and I certainly don't miss having to get washed and dressed every day.' They laughed, Bob was thoroughly enjoying himself.

They walked on up the tree lined lane, there was no traffic because as Eliza said, 'We can travel instantly, we just think of a place that we would like to go to, and we are transported there, because time and space have no meaning here.'

Bob felt a bit bemused, but Eliza explained that when someone dies, they need to go through a process before everything is understood, and Bob had not done that yet. 'It's not your fault though, it's just that people on earth have not advanced spiritually yet, so it takes a bit longer to settle back in here.

Though young children don't have any confusion because they have only recently come from here.

Eliza talked about the others in their group, what they were doing lately, where they had been, just catching him up on the latest news.

As they walked back to the courtyard, they saw Alistair chatting with the others, he stood out from the others because of the energy or light that surrounded him.

It appeared as different hues of blue, whereas the energy fields surrounding the others were more orange yellow and red colours.

They all knew that more advanced souls have different coloured energy fields, from blue to purple with highly advanced souls being of pure white light. Everyone had an inbuilt desire to be like them and follow them on their path of enlightenment.

These spirit beings did not incarnate anymore if they did not want to as they had experienced everything. But they loved to teach and offer guidance to those who asked.

Bob had thought they were guardian angels, but found that the others referred to them as elders. Alistair was not quite one of the elders, but was very wise and could see the best solution to any problem, he and other more advanced souls often gave talks on various topics that the others loved to listen to.
But for now, Alistair had come to take Bob for his life

review.

This was literally a review of the life he had just had on earth. Bob was a bit apprehensive but he felt that he needed to understand it, to understand himself. Alistair had told him that he would learn so much about himself and that afterwards he would have a clearer vision of his future.

CHAPTER TWO

As Alistair stood next to Bob, their surroundings just seemed to dissolve and they were immediately transported to another place. They were in a meadow with grass and trees and there were brightly coloured flowers everywhere. At the far end was a large dome-like building, it seemed to be made of glass but had a more mysterious quality about it.

They walked up to it and through an open archway and into a huge room where at the front was a large screen, similar to a cinema. Bob felt a bit daunted, he knew that they weren't there to watch Shrek and eat popcorn. 'Don't worry you will be fine,' Alistair said.

Bob walked up toward the screen and sat down, he found that it wasn't flat and square but more of a vortex of energy that enveloped him.
He could suddenly feel the life he had just left on earth. He was reliving it all at once it seemed, not just mundane everyday things such as what he had eaten or how he had dressed, but also how he had reacted to situations and how others had interacted with his

own life.

He was not just watching the action, but was drawn in and could feel everything at once, all of the emotions that he had felt, everything that he had said and thought. But more than that, he could feel the emotions and feelings of everybody that he had interacted with on earth.

He didn't realise how trapped his wife and children had felt when he controlled their lives so much. He could feel their frustration with having their freedom curtailed.

As teenagers, they were not allowed out to go dancing or have sleepovers with their friends, he also felt his wife's sadness as she constantly had to reassure him that she *only* loved him.

He realised how he had been so tied up with his own fear of being abandoned, and saw that he had picked up this fear from his own parents when he was a child. His father had left home after many arguments and his mother was so sad and cried a lot.

When reviewing this time of his early life, he remembered forming a belief that others must be controlled to prevent things from getting out of hand.

But he also experienced all the fun times they had, and how his family made his birthdays so enjoyable, how he loved his wife and children and they also really had loved him.
He felt that he could have worked on his emotional

state though and made things easier for his family.

Afterwards, Alistair said, 'Don't worry too much, we are all learning and trying to improve ourselves as we go along.

Your wife and children knew the life they may face before they were even born, and it all added to their own experience.'

It wasn't just Alistair who was there to help Bob, there were also three other older wiser souls. They sat at a table in an adjoining room, they were there to guide younger, less advanced souls in the right direction, to suggest courses of action and give advice. They had white beards and wore long purple cloaks but there was a great sense of peace and love surrounding them.

On earth, they may have been referred to as angels, though they did not have wings, but other souls called them elders. They had experienced thousands of lives in many different places and with many cultures. This gave them a deep understanding and ability to find the best solution for any problem others wanted help with.

Because they had all lived many lives themselves, including challenging lives on earth, they were very advanced as souls and had the ability to know everything about the souls they helped.

Bob and Alistair walked into the room, it was filled with bright coloured light shining through two

beautiful windows.
Bob was asked to sit down and Alistair stood behind him, as he would not be taking part in this discussion.

Bob knew they were wiser souls than any he had met so far, because they were surrounded by a beautiful purple and white coloured light.

They were all friendly and seemed to know more about Bob than he knew himself.

He realised that he had met them before, after completing other experiences and recalled that their last meeting had been about setting goals and overcoming a tendency he had, to control others.

They discussed his life on earth and congratulated Bob on one or two selfless things he had done, but completely forgotten about.
One was when he was younger, he was walking by a bus station, when he noticed some youths laughing at an old man who was standing there, with his trousers down by his ankles, looking rather lost.

Bob had gone up to the man and helped him pull up his clothing and then walked with him to a local charity shop, where they had found him a belt to keep his trousers up.
All three were very pleased with this act of selflessness and Bob was surprised that it had even been remembered, though he did feel happy that he had at least done something right.

They also discussed how Bob could have gained

respect and love from his family without trying to control them.

Bob saw that before he had even been born, he had set a goal to be more respectful of others feelings and learn to be calmer and more relaxed.
He remembered that his wife was a soul he knew very well, she was in a nearby group.
There were five of them altogether and they often joined up with Bob and his friends, doing many things together.

She and her other friends were not as outgoing as Bob's group. They were rather quiet and thoughtful characters and through their experiences together, were working on being assertive. This was because she and her friends tended to let others lead their lives too much during their earthly incarnations.

Before Bob's life on earth, they had agreed to be husband and wife and try to find a balance. On earth she had eventually been assertive and refused to put up with being controlled.

Bob was shown that he could have respected her for this, but chose to be angry instead, so finally, they had separated.
He felt disappointed for having failed a test that he had set himself. He also realised that he had chosen his parents as a catalyst for this change.

'Don't worry Bob, you have gained much in your experience on earth. It can be a harsh testing ground, but so much can be learnt in a shorter time than

perhaps several lives in an easier environment.
You can advance at a much quicker rate, it is after all everyone's goal to experience all they can.

Bob was rather surprised that nothing was mentioned about a promotion he had worked hard for to gain a new job, or his scuba diving certificate that had pride of place in his living room.

They explained that though these things were good for his morale, they made little difference to his soul's growth and this was the most important goal that we all aim for.
For instance, a road sweeper who is kind and helpful to the people he meets every day in his job, advances far more than a high powered executive who treats those who work for him with contempt.

'Your experiences are all integrated when you die, but your ego from that physical life is discarded. We only use it to prove to those left behind that it is really us whom they are communicating with.'

The conversation between them lasted a while longer, as they showed Bob examples of how he could have handled a particular situation.

But they reminded Bob that experiencing life on earth is not for the faint hearted. It is a master class, especially now with all the changes.
But because the spirit world is pure love and harmony, we are very grateful for the chance to live in a different environment where we can test our reactions to all

sorts of situations.

We all live forever anyway so any challenge is exciting. Even just being on Earth now, living through the changes happening at this time is so sought after that billions of souls are there to experience it.

They asked Bob to return to his group and they would see him again when he was ready.

Bob returned to his friends, he felt that there was much to think about and discuss with the others.
They were all very close and supported and helped each other. It was as though they all wanted to grow and advance together, not be left behind. Though he realised that he controlled his own destiny and the others were there to support him.

He soon settled in and had great fun with the others, he met his grandparents and was so happy to see them.

He had spent most of his childhood with them after his parents had divorced and they had made his life a lot easier and happier than it had been before.
They had shared a very close relationship on earth, he had felt so sad when they had died.
They did not look old now though, more like in their mid twenties. Bob found that they were both in the same soul group, so had been soul mates experiencing many lives together.

Those who died in old age now looked much younger,

no one looked old. Who would want to look all wrinkly and frail, though the more advanced souls did have a sort of aged wisdom about them.
Sometimes Bob perceived others as a kind of coloured light and found that you don't actually need a body, you just knew everyone by their unique energy. It seemed to be the older souls though, who didn't feel the need for a body anymore.

Also every soul had a name, it was not an earth name, these were just temporary.

Every soul had their own name, a permanent special name chosen with care, it was given to them at the beginning of their journey.

Some of the names would be impossible to pronounce on earth, hence Bob.

Bob loved to go swimming with his friends, there were magnificent blue lakes surrounded by wildflower meadows and waterfalls.

At the bottom of the lakes were underwater caves filled with colourful plants where they would all swim and play with dolphins and other cool sea creatures, some of which Bob had never seen before.

They could of course swim underwater for as long as they wanted to, the water was always lovely and warm.
Bob loved to swim around at the bottom of the lake, it was covered in fine white sand and there were many shells lying around. They were different shapes and

sizes and some had an iridescence that made them shimmer in the water, it was magical.

Bob watched a small green octopus swim by and thought how cool it looked with all those suckers. It swam down, picked up a large shell and brought it back to Bob. He took the shell and as he did, there was a loud popping sound as the octopus removed each sucker from the shell. That made him laugh as it reminded him of bubble wrap.

The octopus stuck one of its suckers on to Bob's hand, and guided him to the side of the lake where there was an entrance to a cave.
He swam in with his new friend, through a tunnel lined with bright green moss which smelt like hyacinths.
When they came to the end, it opened out into a fascinating cavern.
There were icicles hanging from the roof which shone like diamonds, a beautiful tune could be heard as the water moved around them.

Many different plants were attached to the walls of the cavern. Some had flowers that were like little lamps, where light shone out and illuminated everything. This added some ambient light, as the place was rather dark.
There were other green octopus swimming around, and the one who was with Bob swam off to join the others, showing Bob his friends.

He noticed that there were many more shells here,

beautiful ones of all different colours, and thought maybe the octopus collected them. He loved these friendly creatures.
They all swam down and picked up a shell then brought them back to Bob. The cavern was filled with lots of popping sounds as he took each one.

He hung out with them a lot after this and bought them small gifts which they seemed to like.
They hadn't liked diamonds because of their shape, but when he presented them with coloured pearls, they loved them.They adorned their suckers with a different coloured pearl, and swam around showing them off, they looked so cute.

Someone had conjured up a couple of shipwrecks for interest, and others had added things to the wrecks for fun, so when swimming around exploring, you would come across a chest of sparkling gemstones hidden in a locker at the bottom of the wreck. There were empty bottles of rum strewn around some of the decks, and an assortment of statues lying on the sandy bed.

Many different species of marine life lived in the lakes, Bob loved some large purple flat fish that hid in the wrecks. If he managed to touch one, it would blow up like a balloon and if he could hold on, it would race off around the lake like a speedboat, it was fun to see who could hang on the longest.

There were fish similar to rays but much larger, a big flat fish with a smiley mouth. They were mainly black,

but had a bright green stripe around their edge that shimmered as they swam along.
They were so friendly, and loved swimming around with the others in the water. Bob loved to sit on top of one and it would lazily swim around the lake.

There were also a few boats on the lakes, these had been designed from different eras, so some had old fashioned rigging and others looked like modern speed boats.
There were obstacle courses set up for the boats to go around, and two rainbows to go through which they had to try and avoid, or the colours would become totally messed up.
There was also a bridge with eight arches in the middle of the lake, which they had to navigate through, someone had just randomly put it there.

Bob and his friends had their sailing boat, which they had designed. They had all put their own ideas into how it should look, so it ended up being an amalgamation of all their ideas.

It looked like a brand new modern boat, white and sleek, but Bob loved the old fashioned sails, so these had been added giving it a rather unique look.
They all loved sailing around on it though.

There were also the most fantastic concerts that Bob and his friends often went to.

Sometimes with over a hundred musicians playing many different kinds of instruments. The range of notes were far greater than those on earth, and you felt totally immersed in the whole experience and could feel the music resonating through your soul.

There were operas, rock concerts, jazz and so much more.
These were held in large open spaces outdoors, and the scenery would change according to the type of music being played.

For instance a classical music concert could be surrounded by a backdrop of a beautiful mountain covered in springy grass and trees.
It was totally real, not like a cardboard cutout backdrop, you could actually walk to the top of the mountain whilst listening to the music.
Bob's friends had been most amused when they had first climbed the mountain, because he had bought a few bottles of beer along in case they got thirsty.
He saw the funny side and they did all at least try the beer.

There were many other lovely settings for the various types of music concerts, such as a tropical theme, with beautiful waterfalls and lush green plants, and a band playing lovely Caribbean music. Where you could walk around and enjoy the scenery and music, or dance along with it.

Eliza and Bob loved to come here, because there was a lazy river which ran right around the perimeter.

It was so pretty with flowering trees and huge fern-like plants all along the edge, and beautiful birds and bright coloured parrots perched on the branches singing happily.
They would walk or swim through the warm blue water, dancing to the music as they chatted together.

In the concerts, there could be two hundred musicians playing various instruments, all geniuses at their art.

You could feel the emotion being portrayed from the music and you became totally immersed, you saw in a visual form what the music was saying.

Bob loved the rock concerts, there were many more musicians playing in the bands than he had found whilst on earth, though he did recognize at least three who had been popular musicians on earth.

He had actually been to their concerts during his last life.

They weren't revered here though, or treated differently to anyone else and this was simply because it was just a life they had chosen to have. They still loved music though and continued to play.

They were all brilliant at what they did, the music was so great that Bob just had to dance along with the rhythm. He made up his mind to learn how to play an instrument, as he had always wanted to play in a rock band.

Everyone was thankful that learning was so much quicker and easier than on earth, because you could kind of *tune* in to the instrument and feel at one with it.
There were also many different types of instruments that you could choose to play, far more than Bob had ever seen, because there were a wider range of notes.

Bob also loved to travel and see new places, he just thought of where he wanted to be and so would be transported there instantly.

At first he liked to visit a popular theme park where his family used to go when the children were younger, he thought it was great that he could go on any ride without queuing. But after a while, he got bored with it, things were not as real to him on earth as where he was now.

He had decided to attend his own funeral out of curiosity, wondering who would turn up.
Alistair went with him and they found themselves in a small church in the village where Bob had lived.
He remembered it well, it was where he had married his wife. The old font was still there and the stained glass windows, it seemed like only yesterday they had signed the register on that old desk.

Bob was surprised to see quite a few people there,

including his ex wife and children. He felt deeply moved by their gesture and wondered, if she had died first, would he have attended her funeral.

'They've just come to make sure you're dead.' Alistair said, lightening the mood, Bob laughed. The service was very sombre, far too depressing after all the fun and happiness he now experienced.

He wished that a party, or celebration had been organised instead, but realised that death was seen differently on earth.

After the service everyone gathered outside the church and stood around talking. There were some of his workmates and two of his close friends, plus cousins and aunts, some of whom he had not seen for years.
He went up to his best mate Dan, and tried to talk to him, as he really wanted to let him know that he was ok. 'Dan I'm here, can you see me.'

Bob tried shouting with his thoughts, but it was no good, Dan just stood there looking sombre.
'I can create a white feather, said Alistair. It has a symbolic meaning to some people on earth, it shows that you are here.'

So he chose a woman who he hoped would know the meaning of the feather, and as he created it high above her, it floated gently down and landed on her foot.
She picked it up looking excited.
'Look everyone, this is a sure sign that Bob is here with us.'

'*Oooh'* some of the others said, very impressed.

Bob was happy until Dan spoke.
'It just means a bird flew over and lost a feather, that's all .... What a load of bol..... 'Don't you use that language here,' his wife shouted.
Bob was disappointed, but he knew that he would have said the same thing, though he would certainly have one or two words to say to Dan when he came over.

Alistair laughed, 'Maybe we will be able to arrange something at another time, he said. If you sit by somebody and concentrate your energy toward them, they often feel goosebumps and realise that you may be there.
Sometimes we can influence someone to attend a spiritualist meeting or something similar, where you may be able to let them know that you are well.'

Bob felt that he would like to do that, even though he had not believed in such things when on earth. He knew that Alistair visited earth often and he began to have a real interest in what he did.
Alistair had told him that he liked to help souls who were at first reluctant to leave earth. He had to gain their trust and then he and maybe a family member or friend who had passed before, would be able to take that soul home.

'What is the main reason someone would want to stay earthbound.' asked Bob.

'It is usually where there is some intense emotion at

the time of death, Alistair said.

Not so much fear, but anger or wanting revenge on somebody still on earth, it can take some time to diffuse the situation as they can be very reluctant to move on.
This is rare of course, most departed souls are met by friends or family.'

Bob and his group had all related how they had passed over, most had been met in the normal way, but Clara had an interesting story.

'I was living in a city, in a poor district, it was about 1906. I was already malnourished as my parents did not have much money to buy food and we lived mainly on bread and cups of tea.

When I was about eight years old, I caught Diphtheria that was affecting many children in my town and soon it got worse and I was finding it more difficult to breathe.

Then the next thing I knew, I woke up here, in a sort of hospital but not the same as you would find on earth, there were no x- rays or operations or drugs.
I felt great and the sisters who were looking after me were lovely.
I was told that my energy needed harmonising as I had felt some fear before death, and it was better to do that whilst I slept.

I was soon collected by other souls who I had known before I had been born, and also my sister who had

died as a baby. It was lovely to see her, she looked about six years old and I was told that we still continue to grow up in spirit.'
It was also great that I could go with my sister and grandparents to help my mom and dad when it was their time to cross over. The wonderful look on their faces, they were so happy to see us.

Stan had been repairing a roof and had slipped on some moss and fell off.
'As soon as I started to fall, I knew that I would not survive from that height.

I just seemed to pull out of my body and watched it fall to the ground, as though I was observing somebody else.
I was met by my brother and grandfather, they seemed to appear from a mist and walked right up to me.
They looked so happy to see me and explained what had happened and that I had died in that fall. It was wonderful to see them again.

I learnt that if your life is in great danger for any reason, you automatically leave your body and observe everything from a different vantage point.

You feel perfectly calm, as though you are watching a play, but your nervous system will still react, so for instance you can still be screaming as you are falling. The same thing happens if you are being attacked, you don't want to hang around and feel the pain.'

Sarah had died when she was forty two years old. 'I was living in a city in Argentina when 1 caught tuberculosis and had a cough for many months. I felt weaker and weaker and was eventually confined to bed.

Then one day, I saw my mother, she was standing next to me smiling. She held out her hand and as I reached out to her, the room just seemed to change and we were standing by a beautiful river. I felt so calm and happy, it was so lovely to see her as I had missed her so much.'

Matt told them of his experience which was fascinating. 'I lived in a tribe in the middle of a dense jungle. I was, I suppose, what you would call a shaman.

I connected with the spirit world and asked for their help to cure others in the tribe when they were sick or injured.

I would often be led to use a particular herb or plant and had a lot of success helping them recover from various ailments or injuries.

I was already aware of spirit beings whilst on earth, so when I died of old age, I found myself with my friends here. I did not need to be collected and didn't feel disoriented, I knew and felt right at home, as much of my life had been immersed in the spirit world.'

Most of the others had simply been met by somebody they had already known, because although not many knew much about the afterlife, at least they had an open mind and had hoped for the best.

One or two had felt disoriented and lost for a while, having strongly believed that you ceased to exist after death. They had hung around with friends and family trying to get their attention, but as soon as they relaxed, they were met by others.

If you are religious and believe that you will be met by an angel, then this is what will happen. Whatever makes you feel comfortable and peaceful as you pass from one state to another.

Bob had never given it a moment's thought, he had thought it was morbid to think about such things.

But now, he did feel passionate about wanting to help Alistair with earthbound souls, but did realise he would have to work on his own personal journey first.

Three of Bob's friends came over, 'Are you ready Bob?' They had all been bikers in their earth life, and together they had worked on and set up a large dirt track with hills, bends, tunnels and other obstacles.
It was achieved with thought, they would design a part of the track using their imagination.

The materials though would have to be sourced depending on what they wanted and the track would be manifested exactly how they wanted it to look.

Afterwards they had designed their own unique personalised motorbikes and the four of them had great fun racing around their dirt tracks.

Sometimes one of them would throw in a curveball, and a layer of snow would appear on the track, or a stream would suddenly appear, flowing across another part. They all loved it here and sometimes others joined them.

Bob had been surprised they could even do this when his friends had mentioned it. But he discovered that you can have anything you want, so they created their bikes and the dirt track, and there it was.

It would also stay there for as long as they needed it to and then would simply disappear.
Bob loved racing around the track on his customised bike and as he skidded through some water, he couldn't help thinking, 'If only my mates on earth could see me now.'

Bob did do other things, especially learning to understand himself. Every soul had an inbuilt desire to improve, to become more than they were before, no one remained stagnant and stayed in the same place forevermore. Anyone would eventually get bored with racing around a dirt track or drinking endless cups of tea with their friends.

Bob's self discovery was still fun though, not like

being at school.
He spent time doing this in the library, a modest building with two golden arches at the front. It had a lovely welcoming atmosphere and was just one of the places where souls could go.

It was a fascinating place because it seemed much bigger once you were inside.

There were huge windows and each one had different coloured light shining through. The light rays seemed to harmonise with the subject you were studying at that moment.
There were very long tables that stretched out as far as you could see, with benches running alongside and thousands of books of different sizes stacked neatly on shelves. Every book had someone's name on it.

Bob was shown his books, there were quite a lot all neatly lined up together on one shelf with his name printed neatly on each one.
All of *his* books had a blue cover which seemed to glow, and made them stand out from the other ordinary looking books. Eliza had said that her books looked as though they were bathing in the setting sun so that she could spot them easily.

It was a bright and airy place and had a lovely calm atmosphere.
Bob liked the custodians who looked after the library, there were about five of them altogether, all tall so they could easily reach the books.

They wore long blue gowns that made them look even taller, and they could be quite serious but also had a dry sense of humour.
They would show you where to sit and then find the books that were relevant to you, the custodians knew exactly which book you needed to see next.
Bob could see his own books even from a distance because of the bluish glow that surrounded them.
He could not look at books belonging to other souls, not without their permission, but then he and nobody else would want to.

When he was familiar with how to read them and in which order was relevant to what he wanted to know, he could go and get them himself.

There were books containing all of his personal history from the beginning, each book contained the details of a lifetime or experience and he could see how his future was unfolding.
He could see where he could have behaved differently and what had led him to act as he did.
He felt how kindness and love enhanced him *and* those he gave it to.

Bob loved the library, each book related to a life that he had lived. As he opened the pages, he felt immersed in the story and could sort of zoom in and relive an event that had happened and feel all the emotion at that time.
He discovered that he had experienced many previous

lives, mostly on earth, but not all.

He saw that some events in his most recent earth life didn't in themselves have any meaning, but he had defined a belief about something and then his subconscious mind had agreed, and kept the belief going in order to protect him.
So that, when his parents argued and then separated, he had felt very emotional and remembered thinking in that moment,
'You must hold on tightly to someone you love.'
Then this belief had compelled him to try to control others to keep them in his life.

As he explored the life he had just left, he realised that he had chosen his parents. He saw himself before he had been born, with two other souls.
They were discussing their coming life on earth, and though they were all good friends as souls, they knew that there would be some conflict as humans.

His parents had experienced other lives together that had ended with a lot of anger. So they had each agreed to be man and wife again and try to understand each other, and also more importantly, not to rely on anybody else in order to feel happy inside.
Life on earth was thought of as a role that you were going to play, in order to experience something, and because the memory of your soul life is erased when you are born, you really feel as though it is real, and that it is *the* only reality.

Bob chose these parents so he could experience this

conflict and then try to let go of his tendency to control others. As he explored his other lives, he realised that he had done exactly the same thing in his life before.

As a Victorian father, he had five daughters and had been very strict, regarding what they could wear and who they would marry.

He didn't like them socialising with friends and though they begged to have dancing lessons, he absolutely forbade it.

They had to stay in and do sewing most of the time, or bible studies whilst longing for some freedom to meet other young people and have fun.

He had been far too anxious about his social standing, afraid in case they stepped out of line and damaged his reputation. Far too serious about life in general, and so had ended up lacking any empathy.

Bob's life even before the Victorian one had been quite exciting, he had been a captain on a ship that traded goods around Europe. He had to control the crew, who could be very argumentative, but they worked very hard and their health was not good due to the bad food and awful conditions below deck.

Bob realised that instead of trying to understand their grievances, he had felt angry at them questioning his authority, and he ordered five of his officers to keep them in order.

Bob saw how the tapestry of life was played out, he saw that his five daughters in his Victorian life, chose to be born as his daughters, knowing that he could be controlling, so they could experience what it feels like to lose their freedom.

He found that they had been his five officers on the ship, in the life before, enjoying flogging the sailors to keep them under control.

So their following Victorian life was actually benefiting them, they had wanted to feel what it was like to have no control over their lives.

As we have free will, Bob could have learnt not to be so controlling of others in his Victorian life. If he had let his family have more freedom, he would have learnt a valuable lesson.

His daughters would simply have been drawn to another experience later on, with having their freedom curtailed.

Although he hadn't been forced to have lives on earth, his own soul wanted to experience different aspects of itself and he had been encouraged and helped by the elders.

Bob saw that in another life, he had chosen to be born to an alcoholic mother, just so that he could gain a deeper understanding of living with somebody who was suffering from deep emotional pain.
It was also hoped that his short life would benefit her, to face her fears rather than trying to drown them

with alcohol.

He knew that it was going to be tough, so only decided to stay for a short while. He had died when he was three years old, though he chose to be a female in that life.

It felt almost like being there when he looked at his past lives.

There were no written words in the books, just an immersive experience. He could see everything from a higher perspective, then analyse the problem and see the solution that could have been taken.
He also found that some things, thought of on earth as being punishable, were totally ignored after death.

For instance, being homosexual meant nothing, we have all experienced lives as being male and female. Really, love is all that matters.
As with racism, we have lived with many cultures, in different countries.

Having an abortion was not seen as evil, because souls would know that the woman's pregnancy was not going to progress to full term. So no soul would become attached to the foetus, unless it wanted to experience a very short life. Just to dip its toes into the water so to speak.

Usually what would happen is, a soul who would like to be born into this family, would just wait for the right time and become a child of theirs in the future.

Or the soul would be born to someone who was not

going to keep the baby after birth, but it would be adopted by somebody else. This was a way for the soul to end up with the right family that it wanted to be with. But no one should feel guilty, or believe that they may be punished in any way in the future.

Suicide is not punishable after death, if you feel it is your time to exit, then that is your decision. Though afterwards you may feel disappointed that there may have been a solution for your problem that you hadn't explored whilst on earth.

You may also feel compelled to try a similar life again with similar circumstances so that you could try to overcome the difficulties.

Also of course, the life review will let you to see and feel, the effect that your suicide had on those left behind.

Indeed, many lifestyles can be a form of suicide, eating to little or living on junk foods with not enough nutrients to sustain the body. Working with dangerous chemicals or taking high risk drugs, drinking too much alcohol and many other lifestyle choices can shorten your life.
They just kill you slowly.

Bob heard that the hardest thing you had to face after a suicide were the custodians.
When you entered the library they would say, 'Oh no, we didn't expect you back so soon, now we've got to

go down to the cellar and fight our way through the cobwebs to find your books.'
Bob thought this was funny, he liked their dry sense of humour.

Bob found that the life review was the toughest event you had to face on returning to the spirit world. You relive all of the major relevant events that shaped your life, and not only see everything from your own viewpoint, but experience all the emotion that you may have inflicted on others too. It is a very humbling experience.

Bob had asked what happens to murderers or dictators who start wars.

Alistair explained, ' There is no hell with fire and brimstone and a devil with horns, as they think on earth.

But everyone has to have a life review, so just imagine feeling the pain and anguish and fear that your victims may have felt.

That soul may not go back to their own soul group if they are feeling very angry, but instead will need rehabilitation.

This usually happens in a place where the energies are lower and each soul is totally isolated from others. There are specially trained guides who help these souls to understand themselves and the consequences of their actions.
But in the first instance, these souls are usually

extremely angry and this can be a major barrier for some time.
It is difficult to explain, because everyone's situation is unique, there is no overall plan for a murderer for instance.

Sometimes a soul would be willing to have an earth life, in order to start a conflict of some kind, that will ultimately end up advancing humanity as a whole, but in a much shorter space of time rather than waiting for natural changes to occur.

Or maybe souls will agree to have an earth life, in order to show countries how they are living and hurting each other. As in separation, us and them, this religion not that, class systems, black and white etc.

Those that die in the aftermath, will also have agreed to it, as they know that great advances are often made after a catastrophic event has occurred.

What are sometimes tragic events in earth's history, can also be a catalyst for a change. Often people as a group may be wanting changes in their circumstances and so an event will be manifested that will give them that.

Because it forces people to look at themselves, re-evaluate their lives, realise that material things are not as important as those that you love, and gives them the opportunity to help others.
Or even decide that something should change, that things are not going to go back to how they were

before the catastrophic event happened.

A soul could also agree to be your abuser in a life on earth. There would have to be permissions and a good deal of planning, it would also have to benefit both of you. To take on this role is actually quite a courageous thing to do, because the abuser needs to live on earth, in conditions that lower their emotional state.

So for instance, they could choose parents who don't have the skills or motivation to raise a child and then be born into an atmosphere of depression and lack of love.
When a child's chronic mood state is mainly powerlessness and despair, they may then lash out as an adult, because anger feels slightly better than powerlessness, emotionally.

We have all been abusers and abused, we all want to feel the hot and cold, we are all evolving and having a deeper understanding of ourselves. No one is forced to do anything, but it is the nature of everyone to create new experiences, to become more than they were before.

We can't do that in the afterlife which is a place of love, where nothing is hidden. You can only know things like generosity and kindness and forgiveness etc as a concept. So we choose to go to places like Earth.

Others join us or come into our life on earth and the roles are played out so that we experience what

we arranged before we are born. The challenges and circumstances are put in place, not in great detail but generally.
But how we react to them is what life is all about, there can be many outcomes.

Of course our memory of the afterlife is erased so that the experience appears as real as possible. We are our body and mind, the soul surrounds us trying to keep us on track through intuition or dreams.

Bob had been very happy and excited to experience the lives he had lived, even though Earth can be a tough place, he could learn so much in one life.
There is the intensity of emotions, the adrenaline and fear, it was such a rollercoaster.

He thought it was such a pity, that what we call negative events, were not being done to us by some malevolent God, but an experience we ourselves had wanted. We could then move on from the experience much faster and also be thankful for what we had learned from it.

There are other benefits too Bob thought, such as all the lovely food you can eat.

Because although you can conjure up a pizza if you want, it is not quite the same experience as on Earth, where you feel hungry and can smell and taste and swallow the food, and the cheese dribbles down your chin.

Or maybe feeling cold on a frosty day, and going home to a lovely warm fire and hot cup of cocoa. What a nice feeling as you warm up and feel comforted.

But for now Bob was just so happy to be with his friends with no worries whatsoever, there was no judgement on anyone, no hate or crime.

CHAPTER THREE

Bob sometimes listened to talks given by others, these were very informative and interesting. They were usually held in a large open space, like a meadow and everyone would sit and be enthralled by other's experiences.

Annya had just returned from a life where she had wanted to feel what it would be like to be part of a whole, to work as a group, rather than being individuals. So she chose to experience life on another planet.

'When I was born, my life had already been mapped out, it had been decided where I would best fit into their society, but the role you played usually followed the same pattern as your parents.
My lifetime work was to make clothing, so from an early age I was taught everything to do with that trade, from how to grow the plant to harvesting it and then to making the garment.

You really felt as though you were part of one unit, all contributing to make it work smoothly.

You had no aspirations, no dreams about the future, no regrets, there was no crime, but there was a strong sense of belonging.

It was a life without freedom, but you did not miss that because it was never an option. When you could no longer work, your life was terminated.
Although I did enjoy this life, I much prefer life on earth, where you have so much freedom, where you are truly a creator and have free will. You can design and create your own life, you can travel and explore anywhere you want.'

Bob loved listening to these real life experiences of others, though he knew that it was not usual to have lives with other cultures, until one theme had been explored thoroughly, so that you had continuity.

Life on earth is quite tough because the energy is so dense, and life can be harsh as you feel a separation from your soul.

Alistair had explained this in one of his lectures.

'Your life here as a soul is perfect, you feel loved, happy, comfortable, excited, and there is a wonderful sense of peace. But it is difficult to truly appreciate these things, unless you have experienced the opposite.

So for example, when you have experienced a lack of love from someone, you really appreciate affection and love when you find it.
There are many situations that we are willing and

excited to try, because for one reason we know that we never die, we are here forever.
So one lifetime on earth is a mere nanosecond in our existence.

But also, we all have an inbuilt desire to expand, to become more than we were before, to create, to grow.
On earth, we have the illusion of being separated from our soul for a while, so that we can find our way back, find that connection to our true selves.
Even big challenges are sought after by the soul. If a baby is going to be born with a disability, there will be many souls here who would love to experience that life.

Think about the experience of being homeless and living on the streets, having to use your wits to survive.
You find that you have to dig deep within yourself, to learn how to get food, keep as warm as you can, to find safe places to sleep, how to react to confrontation from others, to stay strong.

What a brave thing to do, but that experience is probably worth four lifetimes, where things ran pretty smoothly.

Sometimes, you may plan an adverse event in your life on earth, because it will teach you something that will help in your future plan.

Maybe you want to be a leader of some kind and that role will require confidence and courage.

So you may choose to be with parents who are rather distant and don't care much about your welfare, you would then have to learn to be assertive and independent, from an early age.

Most of what we can learn on earth, involves our relationships with others, and funnily enough, we can gain more from those that wind us up, than those who are our best friends because;

Those that annoy you, can teach you patience.

When someone has power over you, you can learn how to take that power back.

Those that anger you, can teach you how to forgive.

Someone who abandons you, can teach you how to stand on your own two feet.

When you cannot control something, you can learn how to let go.

If you have a fear of something, then have the courage to overcome it.

Bob joined as many discussions and group chats as he could because he didn't want to mess up his next life, he felt that it would just be a waste. Also of course, there were only a limited number of births on earth, so it was best to make the most of your life there.

He also loved just hanging out with his mates, all

of his group would be what you would call, his soul mates. Eliza was quite special though because she had shared many lives with Bob.

They were sitting on the grass, in a beautiful meadow full of small bright purple flowers, there were other souls sitting around in groups laughing and talking.

Some children were playing with a ball. They were not throwing it, but seemed to move it using their own thoughts, sort of levitating the ball then letting it fly to the next child, Bob watched intrigued.

One side of the meadow was rather hilly and there stood a large outcrop of rocks, and from these rocks a magnificent waterfall gushed out forming a beautiful rainbow above.
The water flowed into a blue pool and children were splashing about in the water, running happily in and out and under the waterfall. They were having a great time chasing each other.
They did not need adults watching over them to keep them safe, because they already had an awareness of everything and were not helpless.

They were not like the children on earth, who had to be fed and clothed and taught everything until they were adults.
They played together a lot but many also stayed close to the earth family they had left behind and also family that were in spirit.

They would continue to grow and age every year as they would have done on earth. But around their mid

twenties, most souls would stop as no one felt the need to look old. Only our physical body on earth is programmed to deteriorate after so many years.
Young children did not experience confusion when they died, because they had not long come from there. They just went straight back to the spirit world and usually a great party would be put on to greet them.

Alistair came over to them, he had come with a message.
'Bob your friend George is ready to come over, would you like to be the first to greet him and bring him back here.'
'Oh yes,' said Bob. He was looking forward to showing George his race tracks and helping him to design a bike. He remembered the races they used to have many years ago.

He went with Alistair to earth and they arrived at a hospital, they walked into a side room and there lay George, mouth open, breathing his last.
'Bloody hell, said Bob, ' is that what you look like when you're on your last legs.' He was thankful that his own face had been covered in mud and grass when he had died.

'Shh, said Alistair, we don't want to frighten him. When you are ready to come over, you become telepathic, he will pick up your thoughts.'
His family have just left for a short break, so this is a good time for us to be here.'

Alistair wanted to know all about Bob's friendship

with George and Ron, as he knew they were very close friends.

'We all went to school together, Bob said. We never moved out of the area so have been part of each other's family doing everything together.

Ron and George liked to brew their own beer and make wine using natural plants or berries, they made lovely elderberry wine, we spent many evenings drinking it.' As they were talking George slowly stood up as his body lay on the bed, and Bob felt a bit of deja vu as George said, 'Is that really you Bob, am I dreaming.'

Bob watched as George went through the process of being integrated. He tried not to tell him too much at this stage, even though he felt excited and couldn't wait to show him everything.
Bob then took him home to his friends so that he could settle in, he promised to meet up afterwards where they could catch up.

Soon Bob, Ron and George were doing a lot together, they had been good friends on earth and had similar interests. One thing they liked to do was visit other planets and hang out in their environment.
The energy was completely different on each one, you could feel it pulsating throughout you.

Venus had a calm, romantic feeling as they bathed in its atmosphere, whereas Mars was more aggressive and energising. Bob and his mates would go and be immersed in their atmosphere for the wonderful experience it gave them.

There were many other beautiful planets they visited, some completely covered in ice, all blue and sparkling white, pristine and untouched with the most amazing scenery. Others were volcanic, with fire and huge jets of steam and bubbling oceans, giving out such power and energy.

They weren't confined to our universe either as they could travel anywhere and arrive there instantly. Time and space was a different concept, there was no need to physically travel from point A to B.
There were millions of other universe's with many different species living on their planet's.
Some species had a vibrational energy that was of a higher frequency than earth's energy, so that if humans could meet them, they would look almost ghostly.

Bob and his friends loved one planet where the inhabitants looked a bit human, but were smaller in stature and had larger eyes and no hair. They were an example of where humans were heading in the future, not so much in their physical appearance but how they lived.

Over thousands of years they had raised their vibrational energy, so that now they were almost spiritual beings like Bob and his friends. But they had chosen to keep that connection between physical and non physical so that they could interact with beings on other planets who were ready to understand the nature of their existence.

Bob could easily talk to them, telepathically of course and was fascinated by their evolutionary progress.

Alistair had been discussing the earth's energies with Bob's group. He pointed out that most people on earth today are different from their ancestors, more empathic and not so tied up with tradition and class.
This is because the vibrational energies on earth are increasing, especially now.

Millions of people have wanted change, as they have observed the injustice of nations and the planet slowly but surely being destroyed. It has taken a major event but it has been a wake up call for many, who have realised that it is our relationship with others that matter and of course the health of our planet.

As people move up into the higher frequencies, their intuition becomes sharpened, they become more empathic and understanding.
Humans are transitioning from being a barbaric race, though there is still a way to go.
It must be understood that we are all one family connected to each other and there is enough in the world for everyone to have at least the basics in life.

How is it right that a few groups have billions in wealth, while children starve to death every day. That so much is spent on the military because nations fear each other.

Nations should come together, much like the United States of America did in the first place. They were once separate states, fighting and disagreeing with each other.
But constitutions were drawn up where each state still retained its own identity and local laws, but they joined together for the common good of the people, for peace.

Children should not be taught that it is a competitive world, constantly competing with each other. To be the best in sport, get the highest results in exams.
Every child is valuable to society and should be allowed to advance at their own pace. Also, if you want them to learn loving values, stop letting them spend hours and hours playing violent games or watching it on T.V

Older people should be valued, they have the wisdom from living a long life. They also have more patience. These values are perfect for raising children. So whilst the parents could continue maturing, travelling or working on their career, elders could be in groups helping the children. It would also stop the loneliness of this age group.

In the past when something traumatic happened, people were so afraid of their reputation and what others thought, that the emotional trauma would be

buried and never spoken of again.
These days everything needs to be out in the open to be dealt with, it is difficult to bury emotional trauma.
This is where the people of earth are now, all kinds of negativity being forced out into the open to be dealt with.

It is all part of a big change taking place.
It depends on the population as a whole though, their overall vibrational energy that determines what conditions are going to be like on the planet.

As earth energies increase even more, they will become closer to where we are here in spirit and so eventually we will all be able to communicate with each other.

Bob and Eliza had been discussing living on earth and what sort of life to choose. Bob was not ready to go back yet, but he had been shown some possible lives that would enhance his experience.

One was to once again be a father with a family in a western society and to try to resist the urge to control others, but it was thought he had a high chance of failure and should try something different instead. He could of course try, it was his choice, but he knew that it was best to follow the advice given.

The other choice was to live in a family unit where the whole village was united and worked and played together.

Where childcare was shared, and problems discussed

and solved not by individuals but within the group, where there was no conflict.

This life would not give him the chance to be controlling, but would have other benefits. He would experience what it was like to live as a large family, all making decisions together, they would be self-sufficient, and live in a remote area where it would be difficult to leave, somewhere like the Himalayas or Iceland maybe.

Bob liked the second choice and felt quite excited about it, he thought about it often.

Eliza was planning a life on earth quite soon, she wanted to be a therapist of some kind, maybe working in mental health.
One of her previous lives had been in Australia, where she had lived with an aboriginal tribe in the desert.
She had loved that life of freedom and missed the huge beautiful landscape and the mystical feeling of the desert. So she was planning to once again live in Australia, working as a healer, only this time she wanted to be a male.

It was felt that the more aggressive energy of the male would enhance her experience with both her work and with the people in that location. It would also give her the chance to channel her energy into helping others.

She was now in the process of choosing other souls who wanted to experience this life with her. Although Bob had spent other lives with Eliza, he was not going with her this time, as he was not ready for another life on earth just yet.

Alistair had explained the process of choosing to be born in one of his talks and many others came to listen, especially if they had not experienced an earth life before.

'At some point you will begin to feel within yourself that it is time to move on, to do something else, we don't just stay here for evermore.

A few souls want to dive straight back into another life, but an average time to be here is about fifty years in earth time. Though of course in the past there were fewer people on earth and things didn't change much for hundreds of years, so incarnations were limited.

When you are ready you will connect with others whose purpose is to find the best experience for your soul development.
They work out all the scenarios that are best achievable for you, as they have a much deeper understanding of you than you may have yourself.

You are never forced to do anything or to choose one life over another, but will be strongly advised all the same and an alternative way would be suggested if it was thought to be in your best interest.
You will usually be shown about three different lives to choose from and some of the people in these lives will also be souls who you are personally connected to.

They will also have to consent of course to being in that life with you and then you all decide on the roles that you are going to play. Everyone will map out their own experience within that life, which may be as a father, lover, friend, enemy etc.

Most of us plan our life on earth adding in the usual experiences. So firstly, the most suitable parents are found who will shape your early life, this is done by consensus with other souls and the elders who will advise and give permission for the up and coming life.

You are all agreeing to play a part so that the whole experience benefits everyone. As souls, we know that we are all connected and therefore feel close and love each other.

So having some challenges in a different environment is quite an adventure. But we want these experiences for the advancement of our soul.

You choose who will be your brothers and sisters and close friends and the relationship each will play in your life. These souls will most likely have spent other lifetimes with you, so that when you meet up again on earth, there may be an instant attraction or a realisation that you somehow have a deep connection with this person.

A loving mate is often someone from your own soul group with whom you have played many roles together in other lives. They could have been a mother or brother or grandparent or lover in other incarnations.

Then other things can be planned into your life, location is important for some and occupation for others, or whether you want great abundance, or will this hold you back.
This is not viewed as important by the soul, though it may be a good test to set yourself in how you are going to treat those working for you.
No one plans their life on earth in great detail, really just major events.
Life is supposed to be fun and we are meant to be ourselves.

Most souls will set a particular time to depart from a life on earth and return to spirit. Many will live out a life until the body ages and then leave.
Some will want a quick exit and so will arrange an accident of some kind, or a sudden illness like a heart attack or stroke.
It's common though to want time to say goodbye to loved ones and be able to settle personal affairs.

If a couple are very close, they may decide to leave together, or soon after one has died.'
In Bob's group, Caroline and James had lived their last life as a close couple, and had decided that they wanted to leave together when their time was up.

So they had planned to be drawn to a natural event that would allow them to die together. On earth it would be called a disaster, but it is an opportunity for many souls to leave quickly together.

When on earth, they had booked a holiday to a warm tropical country and were staying in a lovely hotel. They enjoyed lying in the sun, eating a lot of nice food, swimming in the sea, and then in an instant were back home in spirit.
They had been caught up in a tsunami, but had planned it that way.
Their own souls had planned it into their life on earth as a quick way to exit together.
So they were drawn to book this particular holiday at the resort where the tsunami was going to happen as had all the others who died.

Alistair continued, 'From our perspective, life on earth is seen as a part that you are going to play, an experience to have, and although your life on earth may appear to be seventy odd years long, it is because there is a linear time frame on earth that does not exist here.
So when you return back here, it will feel as if you have been away for a much shorter time, maybe hours.

Also earth is not located in some far distant place, or down below us, but it is here, in the same space but on a much lower energy frequency.

Everything is made of an energy that vibrates at different levels, it is very high here but in an earth experience the energy is much more dense with slower vibrations.

So apart from a few, who have the ability to raise their vibrations, most people cannot comprehend our spirit world or heaven as they call it.

It is rare for anyone to remember heaven, even if they have died and then been revived. But even if they do, there are just not the human words to describe the experience, except as a concept.

When the plan of your life is finalised, you will be shown a sort of screen where you can watch the main points of your coming life. You can view your parents and other relatives who are already living on earth, see what they are like and how they will react when you are born.

Then you can view all the major events that have been written into your life, such as accidents, major illnesses, vocations, where you live, partners etc.

Any major event that we think of as negative when on earth, is not seen that way here, we feel excited by what we can learn from it and how we will react at the time.

When you are viewing these events, you can have a preview of a particular incident, so that you then have the choice of continuing with it.
So for instance, suppose you factored in having an accident or illness that would confine you to bed for some months. This is in order that you now have the time and motivation to write a special book or make

some artwork.

Normally, perhaps you would be too busy, tied up with other things to want to bother about writing, but being inactive will give you the opportunity to be creative in other ways.
So you not only watch that event, but you can enter that actual part and feel the emotions as though you are there.
This gives you the chance to decide if you want to go ahead, or find another scenario that would give you the opportunity to fulfil your plan.

It is common to set exit points into your life. These are what are called near misses on earth, where you were nearly involved in an accident for instance, and you thought, '*whew that was close.*'

Or maybe a major illness has been factored into your life which will give you the opportunity to leave if you want.

These are actually exit points that you planned into your earth life before you were born, it gives you the chance to decide if you wish to continue with the current life.

You may put one or several of these points in place whilst planning your life to come.

This is because life in a particular environment can be harsher than expected, and you can decide to leave if you feel that what you wanted to do is unachievable.

Or indeed, you may think that your life is going to be too easy and more challenges are needed.

There are many reasons why someone would want to leave an earth life, but it's not usually a choice that is decided solely by your ego mind, but more your higher mind and at a soul level.
If you've planned to have a short life anyway, then exit points will not be needed.

As you know, time appears to slow down during these specific times of a near miss.
But what really happens is that time actually stops for you, and you enter into a discussion with other souls to decide on your future, whether to go back and continue with the life you were living, or leave it and return to spirit.

The souls that you meet during these exit points, may present themselves to you in a way that will allow you to feel comfortable. So for instance, you may see the virgin Mary or even Buddha if you are religious, because these are who you would expect to encounter in the afterlife.

Most people though, would meet their spirit guide and maybe a family member who had already passed on.
If you decide to return to your life on earth, then the memories of your prior discussion are erased, you will think that you just had a close shave with death. You will return to the point just before death could have occurred.

Bob recalled his own death, he discovered that during his most recent life on earth, he and two of his mates had gone out on a yacht, just a few weeks before he had died. They were having a laugh and drinking plenty of beer and then Bob had fallen into the water.

He had been dragged out by his mates and everything seemed ok.

But Bob discovered that this was one of his exit points, he could have died and left his life on earth if he had wanted to. He remembered having a conversation with Alistair and two others whilst he was in the water.

Everything around him just appeared to freeze while they were talking.

He had discussed with Alistair and the others what options there were, and the likely scenarios that lay ahead. He knew that deep down, his wife would love to reconcile their relationship and that would make his children happy too.

He realised that he would like this as well as he had felt rather depressed since his divorce.
But it would mean he would have to show some humility and look deep within, learn to let go of his need to control others. He was not sure if he could change, if he was ready yet for such a big step.

So it was planned that he would leave his life on earth,

but not right there in the water.

He would think about his future whilst also being put into a vulnerable position, where he would need to be taken care of and lose his need to control others.

So that was decided, he was going to test himself and try to overcome his fears. As his mates dragged him out of the water, all memories of this meeting were erased, he would have to look within himself as events unfolded.

He knew how that had turned out !

So now that your life on earth has been decided and the unborn baby is developing normally, part of your soul energy is directed into the network of neurons growing in the child and will begin to meld and integrate into its environment.

Your own unique character is mixed with the child's personality, its genetics from parents and ancestors.
In each of your lives, you can take on a different personality.
So maybe if you are an outgoing, adventurous type, but would like to try a quiet, more reserved life, you could choose the genetics of a family whose traits are more like these.
Or maybe your plan is to be a musician, so you can take that energy from the genetic material of a parent who has musical abilities, and integrate it into your own matrix.

As the baby grows to full term, you will only stay for

short periods of time to get used to the environment.

Very few will want the actual birth experience, most join it shortly afterwards. At this time, your memory of the afterlife is slowly withdrawn, so that your experience on earth will feel very real.
There will now be other aspects that you integrate into your experience, sort of layers that connect you and your soul.

So as a human being, there will be your ego and personality or physical mind that come with the body. Your subconscious mind, there to keep you safe from harm, believes what you tell it or program it to believe. Also, like a computer it remembers all of the details as you live your life.

Then your higher mind which connects with your soul and is there to guide you, constantly giving you advice in the form of intuition and insights.
Your life is so much easier and synchronised when you are in tune with your higher mind, rather than letting your ego control everything.

So to summarise, your soul stays here it never leaves, but part of the soul's energy is directed to the human body so that it can experience something.

The soul actually surrounds the body and this is why through the ages you see a halo or energy field drawn around a body.

There is the physical or ego mind, then the higher mind becomes the link between the two, a guidance system that helps keep your life on track.

Then after your life on earth has ended, the physical body is discarded, the hopes and fears and trauma from that life are cleansed away, but the experiences are integrated into your soul. No experience is ever forgotten.

There will be a discussion on how to live the best life as a human, and we will explain how you can connect with your higher mind, as this will be of huge benefit in your life.'
Bob and many others were excited about this, especially those who were planning a life on earth very soon.

He knew that his soul memories would be erased, but he could add experiences into his earth life that would trigger a memory or give him an insight that he was on the right path.

For instance, he could factor in to visit a town at a certain point in his life, and be drawn to a book shop where he would find a book that could change the course of his life.

Or he could join a meditation group and be able to connect with his higher mind that way. Or another soul could arrange a chance meeting at some point in his life, and one conversation could have a big effect on his future.

It was common to set up these encounters with people,where they could relay a message or offer a different point of view just at a time in your life when it was needed.

It was also a way to meet your partner for the first time, you both fix a location to be in at the same time.

Maybe in a certain pub or on a holiday, you arrange beforehand to meet on a certain date, at a specific time and the universe will make sure that it is done.

Bob had met his wife Sally this way, they had set up a meeting point before they had been born. It would happen at a dance hall where they played mostly rock and roll type music.

Sally and Bob both loved doing the jive, and as soon as they saw each other, they knew that they were meant to be together.

CHAPTER FOUR

Things had moved on with Bob, he was now helping earthbound souls who were reluctant to leave their life on earth behind. At first, Alistair had taken him along as an observer so that he could gain an understanding of the situations he may encounter.

He watched from a distance and learnt from Alistair that a great deal of patience was involved. He discovered that you couldn't just rush in and expect someone to go with you, as their emotional state would not allow it. They could be angry or bent on revenge and were often determined to stay where they were.

Alistair would take a look at their life and find a time when they were happy and then try to get them to focus on that special event or place. Once their thoughts had moved away from anger even for a short while, he could bring in a departed soul whom they had loved.

There was one unusual soul they were having trouble

with though.
She was an old lady called Sarah who had died but would not leave her home. It was an old dilapidated cottage that was due to be demolished.
She had lived there with her daughter and grandson, but they were having to move out and were going to be living in an old caravan miles away from their friends.
They were all sad to be leaving a place they had loved for many years.

The problem was, Sarah had been saving money for years to give to her daughter, it wasn't a large amount but it would help her along.
Recently though Sarah's brother had died and had left her some gemstones that he had acquired while he was living in Australia.
Sarah had been to a jeweller to have them valued, and had been told that they were good quality Opel, worth thousands of pounds.

She was so excited, but decided for the moment to hold on to them. So she had put the opel into a small wooden box and then had hidden it at the back of the large chimney breast in the cottage. There had always been a hidden ledge there to one side that only she knew about.

Sarah's next plan was to use the money from the gemstones and her savings and buy a small house for her daughter to live in.
But unfortunately, just as she was about to go and

view a lovely little cottage, she had suddenly died of a heart attack.

She was so distraught and tried so hard to get through to her daughter, but it was useless. Alistair and Bob felt useless too, they knew exactly how she was feeling. She would certainly not leave and go with them, even after their third visit to her.

The next time they saw Sarah was when they were about to move out of the cottage. Her daughter was there looking very sad, and her grandson was with his friend saying goodbye.
They were all packed up and ready to leave when Alistair suddenly had an idea.
He had noticed that the grandson's friend had a dog which had been left outside the cottage in the front garden.
So he managed to use his energy to allow the door to open slightly, and then called the dog.
'Timmy come here, come on boy'

Timmy heard Alistair and came bounding in, tail wagging. The boys fussed over him and were about to put him outside again when Alistair quickly manifested a red ball. He threw it into the fireplace and said ' Fetch Timmy, go get the ball.'
Timmy ran to the fireplace and Alistair quickly told Bob to go and stand in there, right by the hidden box, and try to keep the dog as near to it as possible.

It seemed to be working, Bob held the ball up by the box encouraging Timmy to jump up, and he did so

whilst barking loudly.
But unfortunately the boys went and grabbed the dog as he was getting very black and sooty, and they got the lead out ready to put on him.

Just then the taxi man arrived to collect them all and grabbed two suitcases. Alistair and Bob looked at each other, they threw the ball again, Bob went back to the fireplace, calling Timmy encouraging him to bark loudly.
He slipped out of the boy's hands and ran to the fireplace barking and jumping up and down staring at the bricks where Bob was.

The boys went to grab him again and told the taxi driver that he kept doing that for some reason. Alistair knew that the others would be very reluctant to get into the fireplace to see what the dog was barking at, as it was filthy and they had their nice clothes on.
So he sent the driver a mental message, 'Go and check, go now.'
The driver felt compelled to go and investigate, so he stood where the dog was still barking and looked up the chimney, he just about noticed the small ledge on the side.

He carefully put his hand up and felt around and found the wooden box.
He carried it carefully and put it onto the table. They all gathered around wondering what was in it and when Sarah's daughter opened it, they couldn't believe their eyes.

There was a bundle of twenty pound notes, and four multi coloured gemstones, sparkling in the sunlight.
'I reckon those stones are worth a few bob' the driver said. 'They look like Opel.'
They all looked shocked for a moment and then jumped up and danced around, hugging each other and crying with happiness.

Sarah was so happy knowing that her daughter could now stay in the village with her friends. She was finally ready to go with Alistair and Bob, very grateful for how they had helped her. She could only describe it as magical when she told her friends about it later.

'That was amazing how you pulled that off, absolutely fantastic' said Bob.
'It wouldn't have worked without your help' Alistair said.
He was very pleased with the outcome.

Bob told his friends what had happened and they all wished that they had been there to see it.

Bob accompanied Alistair on a few other trips and learnt a lot about emotions and how they can affect people. He even discovered how strong beliefs could prevent someone from returning home straight away. Alistair had been trying to help a young man move on who had become stuck in a reality of his own making.

He was in a small village where he found himself after death. He was with others who had all belonged to the same religious sect when on earth. They all believed that they were the chosen ones and by following their religion, only they would be saved after death.

They got what they wanted and were all together, congratulating themselves believing they were right. They had been in their small village for some time, still attending their church, singing hymns, having their meetings and feeling very righteous.

But eventually as in this young man, he was beginning to ask questions and was becoming aware of others there in his village who did not follow his religion.
'I was able to get his attention and slowly, he is beginning to understand that everyone lives after death.'

Bob felt happy when the young man and a few others followed Alistair and were taken *home* to be with their families. They felt rather foolish that their beliefs had been misplaced.
But they went on to help others who had judged themselves to be bad people and were convinced they would go to hell when they died.

Bob was soon ready to go out and connect with those souls whose ego's were stuck on earth. He was now working alone, though he knew that if there were any problems, Alistair could always be called upon to help.

He was trying to connect with a young woman who was refusing to move on after she had died. She was trying to harass her ex boyfriend and was extremely angry because he had got a new girlfriend and was now living with her.

She hung around his home creating a lot of negative energy, objects would fly off the shelves and doors would slam shut frightening them both immensely.

When she saw Bob, she was very volatile and he had to endure a tirade of insults. He had been used to this though throughout his various lives, so was quite thick skinned.

He also had some understanding of her problem as he had once spent a short life living with a volatile alcoholic.
Bob knew it was only her physical mind that was hanging around, but it did need to be integrated.

He finally got her to trust him a little and she began to describe her feelings. Bob had been allowed to look at part of her life as he was trying to help her, and saw that she was never meant to stay with this boyfriend.

He saw that they had made a plan before they were born, that when on earth he would be in her life for a short time so that she could experience his positivity and energy.

This was to give her a boost for her next venture in life because he had the ability to install confidence in those he met.

She tended to undervalue herself and lacked confidence. Her boyfriend had helped her set up a gallery and she had begun her painting career.

But when he had left, she had become obsessed, refusing to believe that he was not coming back into her life and then began to hate him and then blame his friends for how she felt. She was extremely angry and began to secretly follow him everywhere.

Her inner being could see that her ego was out of control and for her, there was no lesson that could be learnt from this situation, so the only way forward was for her to return to spirit and reassess the situation.

She had been misusing drugs for some months, so had simply died while taking a larger dose than usual. Bob knew that once she would go with him, the process would allow her to see the whole picture.

Bob told her about his own life which had been rather similar, he could very well understand how she was feeling.
He explained to her that if she would trust him, he could show her why things had changed between them both, why her boyfriend had left.

He finally got her to show him the park, where she and her boyfriend had first met and where they had spent many hours together.
Once she was there she felt a bit happier as she

explained how they had sat on the swings talking together for hours.
At this moment she was no longer angry, her state of mind was calmer and now her grandmother showed up and could finally take her home.

Bob had found it so satisfying to help others in this way. He had needed plenty of guidance and advanced souls like Alistair had given talks and discussions on psychology and emotions and even karma.

Yes a lot of patience was needed as angry people were like cows, Bob thought. They tended to ruminate, where angry thoughts would constantly be regurgitated, over and over again.

He had particularly enjoyed the talks on karma, given by a spirit guide called Cornelius who liked to show up as a hippie with dreadlocks and brightly coloured clothes. They all knew he was an old wise soul though, as his energy was a lovely blue colour. He gave many interesting talks and the others loved listening to him.

A large group of them sat in a beautiful meadow surrounded by flowering trees and Cornelius sat on a small hillock in front of them. He explained what Karma means.

'The belief that someone will suffer in the future if they do something morally wrong, is not really correct. There are just too many variables and so each person has to be looked at individually.

So for instance, there are those who choose to

incarnate together as a couple, knowing that in past lives there had been a good deal of friction between them.

So they keep coming back to earth together, where eventually they will learn to understand each other.

Those on earth though, will just witness the abuse and may believe that some form of punishment will be metered out later on.

As you know, there is no friction between souls, no hate or even irritation because everyone feels connected and can feel love all around.

After any life lived on earth, we never blame any soul here or hate them for anything they did, and there is certainly no reason to ask for their forgiveness.
Because after we have been processed and our fears have been left behind, we can then see the whole picture and realise that we all played a part.

It can be exhilarating and a little scary to live a life on earth, with all those raw emotions and big egos and selfish motives of others.

But the soul can advance so much quicker, than having several pampered lives somewhere else.

Depending on the individual though and their own experience, there could be what we would call a balancing in a future life. Maybe someone overstepped the mark and went too far with the abuse, because we all have free will whilst on earth.

The soul would want to find a balance, and so

the following life would be reversed and the abuser would be abused themselves, the soul would then have had the whole experience and not from just one perspective.

Sometimes a tough early life experience will be sought by the soul, depending on what they want to achieve.

For example, a very talented musician chose a life on earth where he wanted to create music that would have a great impact on humanity.

He wanted his early years as a child to be tough, so that his music would be created from raw emotion from his heart, not from what he could hear.
He was born, with consent, to an alcoholic father who was unable to deal with his own past trauma.

As a child, he had to bear the brunt of his fathers abusive behaviour, and although events could have stopped it at any time, it was not meant to be.
He had wanted this experience, so that his dream of becoming a first rate musician could be realised.

He suffered trauma that caused him to become deaf later, but the music that he created came from the power of his raw emotions, from his heart.
His music would benefit humanity as a whole, it would have the power to have an emotional impact on those who listened to it.
He became a genius and his music still has a great impact today.

So you see, this was meant to be for him, but from the

earthly point of view, it would have been awful to have witnessed his childhood.
This doesn't mean though, that you should just ignore somebody who is being abused.
When anger or revenge are being felt, things can get out of control.

Even one episode can be enough for the experience that your soul had wanted and don't forget the soul is with you constantly re-evaluating your life as you are living it.
But, as in this musician's case, opportunities to stop the abuse were missed because his soul wanted to experience the raw emotions and pain.'

Some of the others joined in the conversation and told their own stories.

Caroline and Robert were in the same soul group and Caroline related how she had wanted an earth life that would be more spiritually based.

'I had spent three lives on earth that were very materialistic.
Money, jewells and prestige had become my main goals in life.
Relationships for me were just a way to gain wealth and once someone could not provide that, I would discard them as if they were trash.
So me and my mentors decided that a more spiritual life on earth would be of benefit.

For me, the best way would be to have an experience

that would cause me to redirect my thoughts and feelings into more spiritual matters, and see that wealth was nothing without the love of others. So it was agreed that Robert, who is a very close soulmate, would be my child for a short time.

He was happy to do this and it would also benefit him.

So I have just returned from a life where my only child died when he was two years old. I loved him and doted on him and was devastated when he died.

But as time passed, I was driven to seek out answers, to want to know what lay beyond and why this had happened to me. I did get some answers in my quest and learnt more about myself and the emotional pain others were feeling who were in the same situation.

I could empathise with them and we helped a local charity who were raising money for a children's hospice.
The experience certainly turned me away from wealth being my number one priority.'

Suzanne spoke next. 'My learning experience covered three lives on earth. In my first life I was a male with a wife and two children, I allowed myself over the years to become angry and irritated by small things that didn't really matter.
I chastised my children and humiliated my wife far too much. So my following life was meant to balance

things out and feel humiliation myself.

I became an orphan in my second life, and from a young age I worked as a servant in a large house where the owners were very wealthy. The mistress of the house never liked me from day one.
She gave me the worst jobs to do and humiliated me every day. I had no other choice but to work there as a slave really, until I died.

After death I discovered that the mistress had been one of my children in my first life. But we had both agreed for it to be played out in this way.

We knew that when we both first met, she would feel some negative emotion towards me. She wouldn't know why, but at a deeper level there was that past life connection.
My third life was spent as a single woman, I had my own places to live, just enough money to get by and a job where I worked alone. This life was created so that I could discover myself, my motives and analyse all encounters.

I never married and could not have children, a medical condition made sure of that. I had friends, but if I became irritated by anything they said, they would just leave and not come back into my life until I had apologised.

It was a lonely but good life because I learnt a lot about myself. I found that my closest friend had been the mistress in my second life and my child from my first

life.
We fell out often because I felt that sometimes she spoke to me with an authoritative tone, and I was also a bit over sensitive, but I suppose old habits die hard.'

Bob knew how differently we see things when we are human, but choosing your own experiences makes more sense than thinking there is a malevolent God that likes to punish us. We all know the environment that we are going to be born into, even animals know.

In fact animals are very tuned into each other and also the spiritual realm they inhabit.

They don't fear death as we do and often wild animals will give themselves as food for another species. This in order that the stronger ones in the herd can continue to keep their species thriving.

If life on earth was perfect, there would be no point in going, our soul is driven to experience all it can so that it will understand itself, it wants to know both light and dark.

Cornelius continued. 'From our soul's perspective, an earth life is almost like planning a dream that you are going to have, it will be over in the blink of an eye compared to your existence which is forever.

Although earth life appears very solid and real, it's actually not.
It is all made of energy, vibrating at different frequencies.

A human body is ultimately energy which has its own vibrational frequency, the same with everything else on earth.
So for instance, a rock has a slower vibrational frequency than water.

There are some frequencies that our human eyes cannot detect, such as ultraviolet light, infrared, x rays, radio waves etc, but they are all on the spectrum of energy.

Our soul does not incarnate on earth, but part of the energy from the soul is channelled into the human body so that it can have an experience from a different perspective.

There is a reason that each soul appears to be aiming for perfection, wanting to set trials for itself in hostile environments and learn how to react in a loving way. It is an inbuilt desire to learn about itself, its motives etc, and then return to the prime source energy, or God as some call it.

God is the purest energy of love, and each one of us is part of this source, an aspect of itself. We were not created out of nothing because we are already a part of this prime source energy. We were each created to be unique and have our own personality.

It may be easier to imagine God as a vast ocean, wanting to explore and experience more of itself. So it took a single drop of water and gave it life and personality. It was also given free will to make its own choices.

So each one of us is part of God but God is experiencing life through us. We are not just part of this source energy. But as we are from the same source, we are all connected, brothers and sisters.

We each have independent feelings and a desire to explore and experience anything that we can think of. We were given life and a destiny to be self guided back to this prime source.
So just as God creates, we are given this power to create our own experiences, to explore and discover new perspectives of ourselves.
Though we will always retain our individuality and not be reabsorbed back into all that is.
Even those wise old souls will always want to explore new ideas.

God is not some pure energy that is remote from us until we are mature enough to re-join it. Any soul can have conversations and advice, or just feel close to this pure loving energy as we do here in spirit.
In spirit, we all naturally feel close to this all loving being.
But on earth all you have to do is *ask* for any help that you need.

You don't need to ask in anyone's name in particular, as there have been many wise messengers over the years.
Just feel that wise old soul as your manager who will help to sort out your problem.

Now put your ego to one side, your longing to want to plan and control everything, even though your life may feel overwhelming.

Let the manager take over, in other words, let go.
Many do this as a last resort when their life is at rock bottom, and you can read thousands of stories of how their life was turned around.

Even without any particular problem, you can ask for the loving energy to be with you.
Many people do ask and can feel the love in their heart, they never feel alone again.

Well, that's the end of this talk, thanks everyone for relating your own experiences, they were so interesting.'
Everyone thanked Cornelius, they would all discuss what he and the others had said, these discussions were given to help them all.

Bob began to miss earth, but then remembered his last encounter.
He had decided to try and give his old mate Dan, who was still on earth, a message just to let him know that he was ok.

There was some preparation to be done first, and Alistair helped him with this.
Firstly they had to influence Dan to go along for a reading with a medium, or somebody who could tune in to the spirit world.

Alistair found an old lady who gave readings and didn't charge much.
So they began to influence Dan to walk a particular route to work, where he would come across her advert.
It worked after a while, he decided to take a different route to work for a change.
He walked that way a few times, seeing the notice pinned onto a door.
It read 'Make contact with your dear departed loved ones. Come and meet Doris, the famous medium.

So he eventually thought yes, I'll give it a go.
So when Dan got home after work, he made an appointment to see Doris the following day after work. Bob called into his house the next morning to check that he was still going.

He stood behind Dan and watched him making a cup of tea. He put three tea bags into the pot and drank two cups before work.

He then called his wife and reminded her that he would be out that evening. *Good*, Bob thought, it's all going well.
So later they all got ready for the big night.
Dan turned up at Doris's address where she invited him in and they both sat at a table.

Alistair told Bob to send clear thoughts to her and not to ramble, so he went and stood next to her and began by telling her that his name was Bob.

Doris, the medium, spoke first. ' Ah I have a man here who tells me his name is Rob.'
' I don't know a Rob, but I knew a Bob who passed on,' Dan said.
'Yes that's it Bob, well he is here and has come especially to see you' she said.

Bob told Doris that he had seen Dan that morning, and watched him making a pot of tea, using three tea bags. He thought that would be good enough proof that he was still around.
She looked a bit confused. 'What's that you say, bags, what bags

Bob tried to shout so that she could understand, 'TEA BAGS, TEA BAGS, in a pot.
'Yes I see love.' she said. She turned to Dan,
'Bob says that you like Tea bagging'

Dan nearly fell off his chair, 'If he's been in my bedroom, I'll kill him' he said.
Bob put his hands over his face and groaned, he tried again.
Doris finally got the correct message, 'He saw you make a cup of tea using three tea bags' she said.

'Oh, said Dan, excited and annoyed at the same time. 'What are you thinking, coming out with things like that'
Doris hadn't a clue, she was listening to Bob.
'Tell him that I have a motorbike and can ride around a track I made.'

She didn't quite understand, so Bob tried again. ' I have a bike, a bike that I ride around a track'

She spoke to Dan. 'He has a tricycle that helps him go around a track,' then she embellished the rest. 'You know, like that old man down the road, it's got three wheels to help him get around. Bob isn't young you know, he's probably got a touch of arthritis in his knees.'

Bob groaned, Alistair could hardly keep a straight face and Dan looked ready to leave.
Alistair asked Bob to let him have a go at conveying the messages, as he could probably send clearer thoughts to Doris.
He told Doris that Bob had a motorbike and had named it vela. *Good* ! She understood and gave Dan the message.

Dan suddenly felt very emotional and tears ran down his cheeks.
He explained that when Bob was younger, he had a motorbike called a Velocette and had named it Vela.
He knew that Doris could not have made that very personal detail up, and now believed that Bob had come to see him.
The rest of their meeting went quite well apart from now, she called him Rob. But they did manage to give Dan some other personal messages.

Bob discussed it with Alistair afterwards. 'Are all these meetings like that?' he asked.
'Unfortunately a lot are, because it can be difficult to

tune in to our higher frequency.
A few do have a gift and if they got the proper training when they were young, they would be excellent communicators, but most don't begin this work until later in life.
They have a natural gift that should be nurtured, but others are often afraid of it, and some even call it, the work of the devil.'

Even the ones better at communicating with us, have a difficult time trying to explain what it is like here in spirit, they can only convey simple messages.
But you imagine what it would be like, if you were on earth, in a room without windows, and on a shelf there is a two dimensional cardboard cutout of a monkey.

The monkey asks you, 'what does it feel like to walk outside.'
For a start, it's not something that you think about, you just do it automatically.
But then what words could you use that the monkey would understand.'

Bob thought, yes it is difficult. How could he explain to Dan, what it feels like to be connected to other souls and the loving energy that surrounds them.
To not be aware of the passage of time.
How you can travel to far galaxies in an instant.
That there are multiple realities.
How you can incarnate into any life form...... This gave him an idea.

Bob, and some of the others, decided that it would be good fun to experience the life of a bumble bee.
So Bob and six others, including Eliza, James and Caroline, sat around one of the large fountains in the square, and discussed what they would do.
They could either incarnate as a bee, and have the whole experience, or their energy could join up with the bee, and they could follow its journey for as long as they wanted.
Bob was up for the second option. 'There is no way that I want to become a grub first' he said.

So it was settled, they all arrived in Cornwall and found a bee hive.
They looked at the bees, found one they liked and channelled their energy into the bee.
Bob was transformed, oh wow, what a different world.
The flowers were not different colours as he had expected, but a sort of ultra violet.
They really popped, stood out above anything else.
They were irresistible, he had to fly down to each one and examine it.

He felt the bees tunnel vision, it's one mission to serve the hive, that was its whole purpose, and It's constant connection with the others.
Bob and the bee flew from flower to flower collecting pollen, then flew back to the hive. Wow, what a difference, it was noisy but vibrant and very crowded.

They seemed to be communicating with vibrational frequencies using their wings, they all knew the

status of the hive as they went about their business.
It was so crowded that another bee bumped into Bob's, and he definitely heard the other bee say something that sounded like *sorry.*
Bees would send messages to the others, keeping them updated about the state of the queen bee.

Afterwards they all discussed their experiences.
'That was absolutely fascinating, 'said Eliza, it felt like I was hunting for gold in the flowers, and didn't the pollen smell nice.'

The others agreed. 'When you flew, did you feel that the hum of your wings sort of resonated with the universe' asked Bob.
James said, 'definitely, but I chose a stupid bee. It flew into a window, I've never done so many somersaults in my life.'
The others laughed.

'I felt that I was trying to stuff as much gold dust into my trouser pockets as I could, said Bob, and then going back to the hive and making it into honey was fascinating.'
'I thought it was like a production line in a factory, with all those cells waiting to be filled with honey and then sealed with wax.' said Alex.
'Well, what about queenie, James said, wasn't she revered, what a diva.'

They had all thoroughly enjoyed their experience and made plans to try out the lives of some other species.

It was not a great success the next time though, because they failed to take something into account. They decided to experience what it would be like to be a fish.

So they found a shoal of small pretty coloured fish in the Caribbean sea.
They each found one and directed their energy into the fish and could then follow its journey.

It was lovely just effortlessly floating around, they were surrounded by many green plants and it was nice munching on those.
Dan thought they tasted a bit like cucumber, very pleasant.
In the distance he saw some bigger fish swimming over towards them, and felt compelled to join the rest of the shoal, where they began to swim in random patterns all together, in synchronicity.

The larger fish were right amongst them now, when all of a sudden Bob and his friends found themselves right back where they had started, in the plaza, wondering what had happened.
They had failed to take into account that they may be eaten for lunch.

Alistair walked into the plaza and came over to them, he wondered why they all looked quite bemused. They all greeted him and related their experience with the fish.
He laughed and suggested that they choose a shark next time. He told them of an experience that he once

had.
He had decided to try out the life of a lovely green parrot.

'I first saw the parrot when I was trying to rescue a soul who was haunting an old pub.
The old man had spent most of his life in this pub and was reluctant to leave when he died. His name was old Bill, and he still sat at the bar smoking his pipe.
The regulars knew he was there, because they could often smell the tobacco that he had smoked.

He was very friendly though and we chatted a few times, he had many tales to tell of the *olden* days when his father had been a smuggler, and ships were wrecked on the coast, sometimes deliberately.

I could have listened to him forever, he was that interesting.
Anyway, the green parrot lived in the pub and could see us. It said '*hello*' everytime we were near it.
So I was curious, wondering what its existence was like.

Old Bill finally came back here with me after I promised that he could live in a pub. So once he was settled, I came back to see the cute parrot.
When I joined with the parrot, a group of sailors walked into the pub, and when the parrot saw them, its whole attitude suddenly changed.

Well, I won't tell you what swear words came out of its mouth, that parrot went berserk, dancing from one

foot to another, calling them all the names under the sun.
Some names I hadn't even heard before.

A few people in the pub thought the parrot was funny, others were shocked.
I didn't stay long, that's for sure, I needed to lie down after that, and if I could have asked the barman for a double whiskey, I would have.'

The others thought this was hilarious and wanted to know more. 'Is the parrot still there and what happened to old Bill.'
'No the parrots long gone, this was around 1940 in earth time.
Apparently the parrot used to live on the ship with those sailors, but the new captain would not let him stay, so the pub had adopted him.

Old Bill came back here, his house looked like an old pub for a while, with its dark wood and horse brasses, he still smoked a pipe too. But he is so talented as a storyteller and is also an excellent narrator, so now he helps produce plays.'

What a great story, they made up their minds to go and see one of his plays.
The others knew that *their* plays usually had a moral story within them, in order to help those who needed it.
But Bob couldn't help wondering if old Bill's plays contained pirates and shipwrecks.

CHAPTER FIVE

Eliza was soon to begin her new life on earth, she wanted to work with those who had emotional problems, and so was taking any knowledge that she could from the spirit world.

She knew that there would be amnesia when she was born, but had factored into her life various techniques that would help her connect to her higher mind, where she could gain inspiration and gut feelings that may help her patients.

She attended a talk about emotions and Bob went with her, he thought it would help with the work he was doing on earth. The talk was given by a soul who had worked on earth as a psychiatrist and continued to have an interest in the subject.

His name was Louis and he liked to wear a dark suit with a red bow tie for his lectures.
He began by explaining that on earth we do not see traumatic events as being positive in any way, we even call them negative and often think that they have ruined our life.

He directed everyone to the range of emotions that are felt as a human and gave the lecture from an earth point of view, since these types of emotions were impossible to have in spirit.

His talks were aimed at adults still living on earth who were suffering from some emotional trauma like depression.

Bob noticed that many souls who were listening to the talk seemed to be a bit different. They had a very narrow stream of energy or silver light that went from their centre out into the ether. Eliza explained that these souls had not died, they were still living a life on earth.

Their inner being was free to travel and experience other things while they were deeply asleep. Many of them were having some emotional trauma in their life and it is during deep sleep that problems can be analysed and solutions found.This is why you can feel better after you have slept on a problem.
Then you can get flashes of inspiration or gut feelings about which direction to take next. Your higher mind is always trying to guide you as it has access to all the answers.

The talk began with a guide to the emotional scale.
'This is an important range of all the main emotions, it is a guide to help pinpoint where you are emotionally most of the time. We all have our ups and

downs but being down near the bottom of the scale most of the time means you are not living your best life.

You have distanced yourself from your higher mind where the positive emotions are, but the idea of listing these emotions in order, is so that you can work your way up the chart.

If you are near the bottom of the chart most of the time, you cannot suddenly make a leap to the top. It will be done a step at a time, but can be accelerated by using other techniques at the same time.

There will be talks explaining all of these.
But important ones are Meditation and Appreciation.

EMOTIONAL SCALE

1. LOVE, JOY, PASSION, FREEDOM
2. ENTHUSIASM, EAGERNESS, HAPPINESS
3. EXPECTATION, BELIEF
4. OPTIMISM, HOPE
5. CONTENTMENT
6. PESSIMISM, BOREDOM
7. FRUSTRATION, IMPATIENCE, IRRITATION
8. DISAPPOINTMENT, DOUBT
9. WORRY, BLAME, DISCOURAGEMENT
10. ANGER, REVENGE, HATRED
11. JEALOUSY, INSECURITY, GUILT, UNWORTHINESS
12. FEAR, GRIEF, DESPAIR, POWERLESSNESS

CAUSES

How do you usually feel, what is your general mood when you wake up in the morning, happy, worried, sad, bored. Look at the emotional scale and try to gauge where you are most of the time.

You will recognise where you are when listening closely to how you feel about something. If your general mood state is mostly on the lower half on the emotional scale, then you will most likely not feel any joy in life and may have been diagnosed with depression.

The trouble is, many of us are emotionally stupid, we bury negative feelings and are afraid to face our fears. If this were not true we wouldn't be too fat, too thin, alcoholic, shopaholics, claustrophobic etc.

Our feelings or emotions should be classed as our sixth sense and be given more of our time and attention.
It is important to analyse how you are feeling throughout the day, to the people you meet and how you feel in their presence, the challenges you are facing and how you feel about yourself.

Determining where your emotional state is most of the time, will determine the thoughts you are thinking and then the words you speak. The trouble is, thoughts are magnetic, if you focus on a subject more thoughts on the same subject come into your mind.

The more energy you put into a thought, the more you talk about it or think about it, the more powerful it gets. So for instance, if you are constantly thinking what a horrible harsh place this world we live in is, your experience will be filled with conversations and other examples to match your thinking.

Your mind creates and so creates more thoughts on this topic, you can become stuck in a loop of negative thinking and this will certainly keep you at the bottom of the emotional chart.
It is so important to focus often on events that make you feel good, such as a comedy show, a family pet, a wonderful holiday etc.
Just one minute of concentrated thought, will bring another thought on the same subject into your mind and then another.

Focusing on gloom for a long period of time will produce a chronic mood state which then causes a vibration that others pick up on.
The energy field that you give out is invisible to the human eye, but picked up by others and along with your body language will give an immediate impression of you.

For instance, if the vibe you are radiating is that you don't feel worthy of being loved, you don't like yourself, then that is how others may treat you.
They will mirror what you think about yourself, not everyone but enough that you will notice.

Each one of us has a past, our own story that plays an important role in our development.
If our past has been full of conflict and sadness, we can grow up full of misery, fear and resentment, feeling worthless, hurt and angry inside.
If these feelings are not dealt with, and repressed like trying to keep the genie in the bottle, they just get bigger over the years affecting our physical and mental health.
It is often why people turn to alcohol or drugs, because for a short time they numb the pain that is being felt inside.

You are aware that you have negative thoughts that you are constantly trying to stuff down, which is a shame because confronting and releasing hurtful experiences is crucial for your future happiness.
Sometimes we want to hold on to that misery because we get a pay off out of it.
Justification for past failures, sympathy from others, wanting to hold on to resentment as in 'he needs to be resented and to know how badly he hurt me for doing what he did, otherwise he won't change'

Often because we are so out of touch with our own emotions, this usually happens on a subconscious

level. The problem is though, you cannot move on if you hang on to the role of playing the victim.
You will think that everything is out of your control and look to others to prop you up. On the emotional chart, this is being stuck at the bottom in helplessness or maybe at the next level feeling slightly better in anger, but not a state to stay in for long.

You may feel justified in blaming someone for the horrible way you now feel, but you cannot change the behaviour of others.
Don't give them the power to keep you feeling depressed, instead feel the freedom of controlling your own thoughts, your reaction to trauma from the past.

If your happiness depends on changing someone's behaviour, then you will never be happy. It will be a cycle of anger for what someone did or said, then resentment and maybe hatred.
Then feeling powerless because you think they have taken away your right to feel good.
You can have all the material things you want, but still feel depressed if your thoughts are focused on hurtful experiences from the past.

Another problem that can occur is, you may in the past have been severely depressed and down at the bottom of the mood chart, feeling suicidal.

But you managed to break free and slowly your mood state improved, but only as far as anxiety on the mood chart.

But now, you are so terrified of going back into that suicidal state, that in order not to 'rock the boat' you try to protect your mental health as best as you can.

So you restrict your life and cut out anything that will induce stress. This may involve staying indoors most of the time, giving up socialising, leaving your job.
The trouble is, you may feel safer, but that way of existing is still keeping you in those negative emotions and certainly not feeling happy.

Feeling depressed or unhappy can occur because of a single event that happened long ago, maybe being bullied at school, even for a short time, a serious accident or illness can also be devastating.
We often seem to look for the worst case scenario when anything negative happens, or think that we are being punished by some unknown deity, or even blame ourselves.

Maybe we are just following our parent's responses to events just as they followed their parents. You rarely hear someone say something like,
'I fell off a ladder and fractured my arm. It was great because it showed me that I had to slow down, otherwise I knew that I was heading for some serious health problems.'

When you are emotionally near the top of the mood chart, you will wake up in the morning and feel glad to be alive. Eager to get up and each day will be like a new adventure, with new friends to meet and great things to create.

Being at the bottom of the emotional scale feels like being imprisoned in a lonely world of self absorption and self defence.

On the positive side though, you wouldn't be unhappy unless you knew a better life was possible.

Indeed, there are those who are very happy with life even though they may have experienced trauma in their past.
So the question is, what has the happy contented person done that is different.

On the emotional code, try and stay in the top five as much as possible, you are closer to your own higher self here and it is giving you a message.
It is saying, 'stay close to me and your life will flow better, you will feel happier.'
If you are feeling unhappy, it is a sign that your higher mind does not agree, that your feelings are misplaced.

Of course there will be times when your emotions will be near the bottom of the chart, when a traumatic experience occurs. But the aim is not to stay there, but work your way up the chart as quickly as possible.

Analyse each feeling in detail, jealousy for instance is driven by a fear of something.
It begins with anger and bitterness and then a wish for another to have less. Though don't confuse jealousy with envy. Envy is a motivator, a natural emotion urging you to strive for more.

Time is a healer usually, but you can accelerate this process by analysing what happened and asking yourself what you have learned from the experience.

If the events can't be changed, don't keep regurgitating what could have happened, if only.
But tell yourself to release and let it go, and then turn your attention to the future.
Anything to improve your mood, except revenge of course. It is ok to feel angry at first, if this feels better than helplessness, but it is not a place to stay for long.

Work with the experience that you have had and find something positive to do. Raise money for a charity, or make a special place in the garden and dedicate that area to the one you loved.
Or give a home to an abandoned pet, go on holiday, anything that will help you find happiness as you work your way up the emotional chart, away from those lower emotions, which do not feel good.'

A lady in the audience asked Louis a question.

'I feel depressed because I have been told that I have a serious illness, why should it happen to me. I am a good person, I often do good deeds.'

Louis looked at her and said 'Think about how you have defined yourself as *A good person,* how you came to that conclusion.
Firstly you had to sift through and categorise many people and then place them into piles of good or bad. So in your mind some went into the bad pile and some

into a good pile, where you have placed yourself.

You are now only associating yourself with the *good* ones and despise anyone who you think is bad. I can see that your bad list is quite long too. Am I right in thinking that you won't speak to the young man living in the next street because he has too many tattoos... Everyone laughed.

At the very least revise your list.
So every day you are emotionally and verbally attacking others and unfortunately that constant destructive attitude has affected your physical body.

We are all connected and some of those *bad* people are the ones that need more of our help and understanding. They can also be the ones who offer us the opportunity for growth.'

FORMING BELIEFS

As we go through life we assign a meaning and an emotional response to things. These are very individual depending on our past experiences and what we have been taught as a child.
An example of an object that would not produce much emotion is a button, to most people a button is just a button.
But what about money, some will love it and earn as much as they can, some will see it as the root of all evil, but money is neither good nor bad, it is there to buy things.
A spider is just a spider, but you may be terrified of them especially if your parents hated them, or you could see them as bringing you good luck if they are in your house.

The same is true of people, you could hate your sister because she got more attention than you as a child, you were jealous and only focused on her negative traits. But the man who marries her, loves her and only sees her good points.

We seem to do this automatically almost on a subconscious level, especially after years of being exposed to negative thoughts or conversations which can trigger an attitude to become a chronic mood state.

For example, suppose when you were a child, you and your family were involved in a car accident, this made you fearful every time you went out in the car and so over time the habit of worry was set, and so your chronic mood state became one of insecurity.
There are many agreements that we may make with ourselves which are totally untrue such as, no one can be trusted, you can only rely on yourself, no one cares, life is tough, money is hard to come by etc.

If you think that an awful childhood is causing your depression, it is only because you formed a belief with yourself at the time. As an adult, you are now free and safe, so what have you hung on to?
Think of this, as a child, the person who is supposed to love and nurture you, often calls you a stupid idiot.
You feel angry and every time you make a mistake, you believe that you are stupid. Because of this constant lack of love and care, you then begin to believe that you don't deserve to be loved.

You are likely to have learnt things that may help in your future, such as assertiveness or problem solving, or independence etc, which was the aim of your life. But other false beliefs need to be dealt with.

The subconscious operates on the principle of suggestion, when we talk to ourselves, the subconscious listens and accepts what we say to ourselves as true.
It also registers the negative things we think about ourselves and accepts them as reality as well as our wishes and hopes, it responds to the emotional meanings of words.

The stronger the emotion, the more impact it has at a subconscious level, but also the more we repeat something to ourselves, the more impact it has. Simply put, this is what happens. First there is a thought, then an emotion and finally a belief.

Thought - That cow over there looks angry
Emotion - I'm scared
Belief - Better avoid all cows, they are dangerous

So that in the future whenever you come across a cow, your subconscious mind will suddenly alert you to protect you from harm. Adrenaline will be pumped into your bloodstream to give you the energy to run as fast as you can.
But someone else could think, Aaahh, the mom is protecting her calves, better give them plenty of room. Therefore no belief.

Thought - I may be made redundant
Emotion - I'm very worried
Belief - I won't be able to pay the bills

Or

Thought - I may be made redundant
Emotion - relieved
Belief - I have the opportunity to re-evaluate my life and hopefully start my own business

The trouble is, if we hold onto or dwell on the negative beliefs that happened back then, or feel resentment or anger, we continue to hurt ourselves and our mood will be at the bottom of the emotional scale.
The past is gone, no good resenting it, on some level you wanted the experience, and by that I don't mean your ego, but more on a deeper soul level.

You often find that many of those people who we consider great or influential, had a rough childhood. But from neglect one can learn self sufficiency, independence, the drive to succeed and take risks and also the ability to empathise with others in similar situations.

What these people seem to have done is turn anger into aggression. Aggression is misunderstood, without it we would do very little in life.
It gives us the impetus and drive to push forward, to take risks, to be assertive, to defend ourselves if we are being taken advantage of.

Violence is not the same as aggression, it is actually passive. What happens is, we have held onto feelings of anger, hatred, guilt or any of those lower emotions.

Then some event causes those feelings to come to the surface and we suddenly release them and let all the anger go.

This makes us feel better emotionally for a short time, but unless those underlying fears are dealt with, we just end up in a continuous cycle.
It's not about changing your mind and thinking 'what they did is ok.'
Instead, release the poisonous anger within your mind and body because holding on to it can cause us to attract similar relationships and situations.

So to feel happier, the first thing to do is to set the intention to let go of negative beliefs and see resentment and anger as toxic to your physical and mental health. Tell yourself and mean it, that you want to replace these emotions with good health and peace.

You will be putting that intention to your subconscious mind, so just relax and let it do its job. Be aware of anything that comes into your life that may help with your situation. You may be drawn to something unusual, it will seem to jump out and grab your attention.

Then follow the series of exercises following and you will work your way up the emotional scale one step at a time and as you do, the memories of pain and fear and hurt, will fade away.
Those negative emotions will be replaced with more positive ones, then as you begin to feel happier, your

inner mind will dictate how you then feel outwardly.

It will not take as long as you think and once you are in tune with your feelings and can control them, nothing will ever affect you in the same way again.

Yes there will be challenges and obstacles that come along because we (our higher mind) do not want a totally boring life where there are no challenges, nothing to aim for. But when you are mainly happy with life, you are rarely affected emotionally for long when an unhappy event occurs.

Be grateful for the experience, as adversity can force you to explore the creative role of having a positive attitude, which can free you from the past as it is directed toward the future.

Firstly do not feel guilty about being depressed, yes it may affect others close to you and then you may feel guilty and upset with yourself, but the past is gone, you want to turn your life around and are willing to get started.

Say out loud three times, 'I am where I am and it's OK' and it is OK.
You are actually very brave to have gone through the trauma and come out the other side. Try to accept the event as an opportunity for growth.

CHAPTER SIX

SOLUTIONS

First of all you will need a notebook and pen, it is best to keep everything private that you are going to write about. This is because when you discuss personal things with others, you will get many different opinions and the point of this exercise is to get to know yourself.

When you wake up in the morning, spend a few minutes writing about how you are feeling emotionally. Do you have nervous feelings in your stomach, do you feel angry, are you tensing any muscles, are you dreading the day ahead.

Try to pinpoint in your body where you feel any negative emotion and describe what it feels like. Feeling the emotion will lead you to question the belief behind it.
So for example, if you feel inferior or unworthy, really feel that emotion and ride with it, let the emotions flow.
Look at the mood chart to help with describing

the way you are feeling and be totally honest with everything you write down.
Next, try to narrow down reasons why you may be feeling this way. What do you generally worry about during the day?

As you go through a typical day, analyse everything in detail and write down anything that makes you feel unhappy. Include work, is it the long hours, the journey to get there, the people you work with, the wages etc.
How do you feel at home, loved, taken for granted, appreciated, safe, overworked.
Find the emotional feelings on the chart, for instance, you may be in a situation where you think nobody appreciates what you do, how hard you work, you may feel like a doormat.

So decide on the chart which emotion you are feeling, it may be unworthiness.
Do you spend time thinking about something that happened to you in the past.? Write down all your feelings and become aware of your general emotional state.

Next, make a list of all the significant people in your life, past and present. Include those you have loved, hated, feared, appreciated, anybody that has played a role in your life.
Now use a separate page for each person and for each one, write down your overall impression of this person.

Be honest, don't feel guilty, include their character, how they interact with you, their good points and bad points, how you felt or feel in their presence. Do you feel relaxed, loved, on edge, jealous or irritated etc.

Look on the mood chart and try to judge how each one generally feels and how you feel when in their presence.
If an event happened that you did not like, write about it, do not be afraid to go through it again, it needs to come out into your conscious mind to be dealt with.

Write in detail what happened, your emotions at the time, how you reacted, were you allowed to show how angry or hurt you felt, were you supported by anyone else.
How do you feel about it now, are you letting it control your thoughts and therefore your mood.
Keep it simple though, you don't want an epic of war and peace on who did what and when. As well as faults, describe their loving qualities, what others find attractive about them.

If someone has hurt you in the past, shut your eyes and imagine that person standing in front of you looking down at the floor. Now talking out loud, say how you felt, what you think of them. Get everything off your chest, shout, feel the anger, listen to its power and fury, let all the emotion out.

You may then want to ask, why? This is a question we all ask when some tragedy happens, because we think that knowing why something happened will help us

to understand it.
The trouble is though, we tend to keep our feelings and emotions in check and spend little time analysing our emotional state.

So there isn't much chance of getting an answer to that question.
Often the person who hurt or abused you, were themselves treated in a rough way when they were a child and learnt that violence was the way that negative feelings were dealt with.

As an adult, it is then difficult to cope with the stress of parenting and a child may be a reminder of their own sad childhood, of the powerlessness that was once felt.

This usually happens on a subconscious level as the emotions were suppressed and so any stressful situation causes anger to be felt. Unfortunately, this can be repeated through generations of the same family.

Other events such as accidents may also not give you the answer of, why has this happened to me. Because our physical mind is sometimes not meant to know. Our inner being or soul, the real you, has set the experience up in order to learn from it.

Whatever the traumatic event is, doesn't matter to your soul, it is your long term reaction to it that is important. So to help reduce the impact of it, continue

with the exercise.
If the trauma involved someone else, take your pen and paper and draw a picture of that person.
Make it a cartoon character, use your imagination. For example, put a dummy in its mouth, put a bunch of bananas for hands. It could be a mouse, cat or bird or the devil etc.
Now as you look at this picture, write down how you felt about the situation. Now put into words how you would have liked that person to be, what the relationship between you feels like if it had been different.

Then write down, is there anything further that could help me with this, relax and write down anything that comes into your mind, don't analyse it just write, often you will gain some insight.

Finally write, and say out loud, I choose to let these feelings go, I choose to release all anger, all sadness, all resentment and guilt, it is safe to let them go.
You are talking to your subconscious mind

Now make a pact with yourself, that you are going to erase the pain of that event from your life. All those feelings of fear, resentment, anger etc, don't belong in your life any more.
They are like an acid, eating you away bit by bit and as long as you hold on to the pain of the past, it continues to live and hurt you.
It's time to say, enough is enough, I am going to let the past go and I will practise being loving and kind

to myself. I will value my life, I am unique and have gained much from my experience.

Now go and burn those notes you have written or tear them into shreds and get rid of them, vow to move on with the rest of your life and trust that it will get better. Just focus on what you now want and give your attention and energy to that. Start doing things that make you feel happy.

If you have long term depression but cannot think of any reason why it started, it may be that something happened when you were a baby. We rarely remember that far back. Maybe your mother had postnatal depression and you were neglected for a time.
As a young child, you are very emotionally connected to your parents and can pick up on their feelings far easier than when you are older.

Do the exercise above as it may give you a chance to focus on how you interact with the people in your life. Write down any fear or anxiety you have. Go into as much detail as you can, whatever comes to mind, what exactly are you feeling.
See if you can pinpoint in your body where you feel that emotion, does it have a colour or shape, how strong is it.

Feel that emotion, make it as strong as you can, then say to yourself
'I release and let it go, it's safe to let it go, all the pain, all the sadness, all the fear, it's safe to let it go.

Now feel that emotion again of fear or anxiety or sadness, whatever it is you are feeling and then say to yourself 'I choose to let go of all feelings that I am a failure, that I am not good enough, that I am stupid, it is safe to let them go'
Keep repeating this, feeling the negative emotions first, you can add your own words as you may have different views about yourself.

Now shut your eyes and imagine that a child is standing in front of you.
The child is you, still very much a part of yourself. Talk to him/her as you would talk to a five year old, tell her you love her and give her a hug, then ask her if there is anything she would like to say to you. Just relax and listen.

It is important to monitor your thoughts and feelings as you go forward and not to fall back into those old thought patterns. So at first, make notes every day of your experiences, your thoughts and feelings and the actions that you took.

The way to transform negative emotions is not by trying to fight them or suppress them, but instead by replacing them with something more positive.
By changing your attitude to a problem, you are adding your own creative energy to the situation which will help transform it and displace it.

Look at a problem you have and make a note of how you usually feel toward it. Do you feel angry

or disappointed and maybe powerless because you cannot change the situation?
If instead you develop a caring attitude and hope for an optimistic outcome, you will displace those feelings and your energies will be guided to a more loving solution. Say 'I release fear and all is well'

Develop a forgiving attitude towards yourself and others.
Get into the habit of writing down everything about the situation and ask for a solution. You could go more general and write or simply ask out loud, 'what does the fulfilment of love look like in my life, what would I have to give up or release in order to manifest this vision.'

Write anything that comes into your mind however daft it sounds, then observe your thoughts for the next few days as there may be a delay in your perceiving the solution.
You may be drawn to go out for a walk and while you are relaxed, may receive a flash of inspiration, or randomly meet someone who gives you some good advice.

Never forget that, no matter how oppressive a situation is, nothing can take away the fact that you can choose how you will respond.
Simply by asking what you can learn from a bad situation, you have changed your attitude. You are no longer focusing on being the victim, you are taking control, being creative, becoming self aware.

Here are some examples of how to change a negative situation with a caring attitude.

Firstly, make a list of any positive traits that a person has who is annoying you. Even if you can only think of one, such as they wear nice clothes.
Or make one up if your only thought is, 'I would like to drown the stupid idiot.' Then only focus on these positive things when you think about or see that person.

If it is a partner that you resent at the moment, put up photos of when you were happy together and look at those often and feel the happiness you had, focus on the good times especially when you feel annoyed with them.

Instead of directly attacking someone verbally about something they did or didn't do, talk about how it made you feel. Approach things with an attitude of love.
Love yourself, care about your health and respect your limitations. If you feel guilty about the past, forgive yourself, the past has gone.
Write down all the things you love about your work and write about a perfect day or perfect week, what does it feel like.

Practise feeling worthy by accepting positive comments from others. Try asking for small favours at first, just to build up your self esteem. You are just making requests not demands, so don't fear rejection.

Take charge of inner conversations that are just plain wrong.
Such as, *I am not good enough, I am a failure, I don't deserve to be happy.*
They were set by the child and even though you are now an adult, they are working in the background, sabotaging your relationships or career.

Often a good indicator of how you really feel inside are your friends and colleagues. One or more will act as a mirror and treat you in the same way that you are feeling about yourself. So for instance, do you put yourself down, think you are not good enough, don't deserve anything nice.
If others show you no respect or love, take a look at yourself and the vibe you are putting out.

Maybe that enemy of yours, is more of a teacher, pointing out that your beliefs are all screwed up, mirroring what you are feeling about yourself.

The people we usually dislike are often the ones that help more with our development, as we live through that experience, being there, feeling it, making emotional choices on what we did or did not like etc.
This is why you usually cannot change another person in the hope that you will feel better, because as long as you feel self loathing, others will continually come into your life and treat you in the same way.

You must change yourself first and when you set the intention to do that, everything in your life

will automatically change, you should feel love and respect for yourself, confident and eager for the future.
It is important to decide who you are and then accept it.
If you are naturally an introverted person who prefers a quiet life, or an extrovert who likes to party. Then this is who you are and you are perfect.

Don't feel disappointed with yourself for as long as you reject or deny who you are, you will always be in conflict with yourself which will then cause anxiety. We tend to beat ourselves up about our body shape, our looks, how we have lived our life etc. It is time to stop feeling unworthy or less than anyone else.

Make a list of anything that you like about yourself, it could be your hair, skin, health, whether you are truthful or independent.
Ask friends what they like about you, then only focus on these good qualities especially when you find that those negative thoughts are creeping in.

As you begin to feel better about yourself, change your surroundings to suit your more positive attitude. Watch more comedy and light hearted programs and reduce any negative input like newspapers, programs about conflict, anything that lowers your mood.

Get rid of anything that isn't working in your life. For example old love letters from an ex, a friendship that isn't working out, clothes that you haven't worn for at least a year. You must let the old stuff go, before new things can come into your life.

Drop any friends that use you, who don't support you and choose happy positive people who share your values and goals. When you go out, walk upright, don't slouch, and smile at others, you will soon make new friends.

If you want a so-called friend in your life but who does not support you, maybe criticises you, controls you or puts you down in front of others. Let them know how their behaviour is making you feel.

Don't be afraid to ask your friend why they criticise etc.
Don't get angry though, leave the emotion out of it.
After thinking about your question, which may take some time, your friend may realise that there is a deep seated reason for their behaviour toward you, it could be jealousy for instance.

It may feel better to know that you have done everything you could to solve the problem, rather than say nothing and let resentment eat away at you.

Often others don't even realise they are treating you in this way, they are acting from their own fear. Also again, write a list of your friends positive characteristics and focus on those wherever you can.

In conclusion then, appreciate what is happening, investigate why you are reacting the way you are. Get in touch with whatever belief system is generating that particular reaction.

Find out what it is consciously and when you believe it doesn't serve you anymore, add that energy to the great unique experience that you have had, and then manifest what you prefer.

Feel and see yourself in that visualisation, already living that, and feel how exciting that is to you. Think, feel and behave as your future self, say often,
I am always positive
I expect to win
I believe in myself

CHAPTER SEVEN

Bob had listened spellbound to this information, he wished he had known this in his last life on earth, and thought that it should be taught to teenagers, when they are about to become adults.
It is at this age that emotions are near the surface and for a very good reason, they are there to be dealt with and released. The young person can then begin adulthood without carrying any fear or anger from their childhood.

He remembered his own teenage years, rather turbulent but exciting.
A sort of angry feeling deep inside with society as a whole, an attitude of, 'You're not gonna tell me what to do or how to behave.'
He had gotten tattoos, grown his hair long, bought a motorbike, smoked a bit of cannabis now and then and had a good time with his mates rockin and rollin with the girls.

As a soul, he still liked to ride his motorbike around the race tracks, his friends were continually changing the layout of the tracks to keep them interesting.

But he didn't do it so much now, he was beginning to feel a bit restless.

He was still going to earth and helping earth bound souls, in fact the one he was trying to help now was being very resistant.
He was a young Scottish man named Alex, who was hanging around an old fort that had once been used by the British military.

During Alex's last life on earth, it had been a very turbulent time with much friction between the British and Scots.
He had been part of a clan who loved their way of life, living in groups, being self-sufficient, and having a great heritage that went back many years.

But the clans knew that the British were trying to destroy their culture and they tried to fight back as much as they could. Alex was very vocal and persuaded other clans to join together, where they planned attacks on the troops.

There were many skirmishes and the clans were becoming a real threat, as they gained more support in their fight against the British.

But Alex himself was caught one day, and as a deterrent he was taken to the gallows and hung.
His body was strung up in a public place, as a warning to the others, if they continued to resist the British.

As Alex was being led to the gallows, he put a curse on them all, and vowed to haunt them and anyone else

who came to live in the fort.
He had certainly kept his word and people did occasionally see a young man wearing a kilt wandering around the fort.
In Alex's mind, he was still trying to protect his people and their way of life, he still felt angry and was determined to stay there.

Bob was having trouble even getting close to Alex, he would simply rush right through Bob and go somewhere else, he had no idea that over two hundred years had passed.

Bob and Alistair decided to try going in a group rather than on their own.
So they also asked Cornelius, as he had a wonderful calming energy, that would hopefully calm down even the most angry soul.
They decided to appear dressed as a clan group and to appeal to Alex to help them, as if they were being pursued. This they hoped would get his attention.

They got themselves ready, though it was rather amusing to see Bob wearing a kilt, as it didn't quite suit him. They also took three horses to look more authentic, and then stood by the fort entrance and called for Alex's help... *Great* ! it seemed to be working, he came down to the entrance.

' Och, I see you are with the MacDonald clan. Watch your backs, the British could be back at any time, I'll kill the bastards, snap their wee necks.'

Alistair spoke, 'We heard you were here Alex, we're travelling up to Skye and needed a guide, we were told you could help us.'

' I'll no be leaving here, gotta protect my own kin'
' We haven't got the strength and courage that you have, we might be attacked by the British, we need your help.' said Alistair.

'Och, yer talking oot yer arse, there's three of yer, I canny leave here.'

' Well if you're sure, we'll be leaving then. But we asked Isabella to meet us there, we thought that you would love to see her,' said Cornelius.

'No !!! my bonnie lass Isabella, I haven't seen her for so long. We were to be wed when I returned.

'The British troops are in London, they won't be back here for some time. Come to Skye to be with her, you can come back to the fort later,' said Alistair.

'I do so miss her, I dunno,' said Alex.
He looked back at the fort. Alistair had never known anyone as stubborn as this.
'She'll only be there for a wee while, so if ya don't come now you'll not see her again.'

Eventually Alex agreed to go, they mounted the horses and set off along the road. Very shortly they arrived on *Skye* and came to a small clearing in a forest, where there stood a charming small cottage with red roses climbing over the front.

Standing by the door was Isabella, they ran toward each other and Alex hugged her as though he would never let her go.
They felt so happy to be together.
The others left, very pleased with the outcome. Bob was very happy, he loved this job of helping others, he planned to come back and see Alex when he had settled in.

Bob had discovered a new hobby which was keeping him well occupied.
It was painting, there were many galleries where art work could be displayed and it was an incredible experience to wander around and immerse yourself in each work of art.

You could really feel what the artist was trying to convey in their artwork, what emotion and energy each picture portrayed.

Bob liked to try and show speed and energy in his work, so of course he had a few paintings where motorbikes were racing around a track.
They were very good because of the wider range of colours and hues that he could choose from.
It also seemed much easier to put the emotion of what he was trying to show in his artwork.

He also loved painting pictures of the solar system, especially planets around earth. The others loved his picture of planet Mars with all the beautiful reds and oranges, and could pick up the vibrancy and energy of the planet when they looked at it.

Doing any sort of artwork was purely a hobby, something that you loved to do.
There was no need for money.
Rosie, who was a close friend of Bob's, liked to design clothes.
This had been her job on earth and she still loved doing it, even more now with the incredible range of materials, including a lovely silk like fabric that was very popular.

When you had just returned from your earth life, you automatically had the most appropriate clothing on.
But afterwards you could dress however you liked, so every soul looked different.
Some loved the ancient Greek style of clothing and some loved the Victorian style.
Other groups liked to keep to the traditions of a life that they had shared together, so Bob had found a group of friends who were dressed in Japanese apparel.

Souls would go to someone like Rosie and she would design and make an outfit for you, not with a needle and cotton, but it was more of a thought process and a collaboration between the two of you.
Bob sometimes came across souls who didn't feel the need to present themselves either with clothing or even a body.

They looked like a strip of coloured light or energy,

but everyone automatically knew who they were. Everyone's energy was different, not a block of one colour, but many shades and hues forever changing as they evolved. Bob's energy was various shades of orange with a bit of red.

Quite a few professions were still pursued if you had loved doing them on earth, or didn't have the opportunity. Maybe, writing plays or Poetry, singing, playing an instrument, nursing, as in helping to align a souls energy, teaching, tailoring and even architecture.

Bob had found someone who loved designing different styles of buildings to live or work in.
He had gone to see how Alex was getting on and found him in the lovely little cottage surrounded by a magical green forest. He was talking to Isabella, who was one of his soul mates.
They greeted Bob like an old friend, as to them he was. They were so grateful for the work that he did, and Alex told him what had happened since he last saw him.

'Well, I've been looking at my past and found that I had another life living in Scotland. That's why I had such a passion for the place, I am also discovering a lot about myself.
I love Scottish music, bagpipes and such, so I help organise a large band of musicians, and me and Isabella go and have a great time dancing the Gay Gordons.

Isabella is trying to teach me another skill. She helps to design buildings, and wants me to come up with some ideas so that we can make this cottage a bit bigger.'
' Yes and so far he has designed a room that looks like a pub with a dance floor' said Isabella.' They all laughed.

After a chat they all went outside, it was just beautiful being amongst the trees, you could feel their energy, as if the leaves were trying to hug you and protect you. They walked out of the forest and down a country lane, where at the end was a small town that stood on the banks of a river.

It was so pretty, there were many different sized buildings. All were designed to be unique but to fit in with the landscape.
Isabella was actually one of the architects who had helped to create this town.
She pointed out two of the smaller buildings that she had designed herself.

One was a very pretty house which was quite small and narrow. It had four windows each with a window box where dark red plants trailed down, setting off the light green colour of the building.
The other house was larger but was a pale orange with four white windows. All of the building's in the town were different, all painted in various light colours.

They fitted in so well with the rest of the landscape, and did remind Bob of a place he had visited in

Scotland once. Though here, the atmosphere was magical, it all blended together in harmony.
He loved it and was most impressed.

This place was different to where he lived, where the town was set in courtyards with fountains and the buildings had a pearly luminescence about them.
Isabella also described how she was helping to design some dome-like houses made with a type of glass, which fitted into a landscape of snow covered mountains and trees.
These souls had lived in areas like Norway or Iceland on earth, and felt happy in this type of environment.

There were many different types of places that souls inhabited. Some even lived in mud huts with straw covered roofs, in the middle of a desert.
Isabella had visited the place once. 'It certainly wasn't a barren place she told them, there was a beautiful blue oasis lined with palm trees, where you could swim with amazing coloured fish.

There were exotic plants with beautiful vibrant flowers everywhere, and huge animals like tigers and elephants and giraffes, roaming around.

Everyone interacted with them, they were all perfectly happy, like one big family.
I even swam with a hippopotamus which was amazing.'
'Ooow, we must all go and visit.' They made plans to go and see the place together.

Bob became good friends with Alex and the other six in his group. One of their characteristics was that they showed a high degree of loyalty toward one another, during their incarnations.
This quality was attractive to Bob who had the tendency to want to force others to be loyal to him, during his earthly lives.

He liked to go snowboarding with them down one of the nearby mountains.
They had set up a cable car to take them to the top, it was more fun than just suddenly appearing at the summit.

Once, Alex had decided to speed up the cable car, where it had zoomed to the top of the mountain, rocked violently and threw them all out. Bob forgot that he was already dead and actually checked his trousers.
The others thought that was hilarious, they warned him that Alex was a bit of a joker.

They told him how they had been snowboarding down the mountain, expecting to go to the bottom, but had ended up at a pizza hut instead! Bob laughed, he could just imagine their surprise.

Their various Groups often joined up where they played together, or discussed their experiences with each other.
His motorcycle race tracks had now become a proper circuit with many more obstacles.

There were balloon-like spheres, full of glitter, that floated around the tracks. You had to avoid them or they would burst, covering you with glitter.
You would sparkle for some time, and this would distract those trying to study in the library.

There were more ramps, where you literally flew over the top and landed on the other side sometimes after doing a somersault.
One ramp went right over the top of a building, and then, you had to avoid a pond full of tomatoes on the other side. Alex had designed it and yes, you guessed, the building was a pizza hut.

Bob learnt so much from the others, their journeys were fascinating to listen to.
John and Maryann had been horse dealers during their last life in Victorian England, they had loved their work and had developed a special bond with horses.
So it was natural to continue with their interest.
They had a meadow in which many horses happily roamed. Anyone could come over and choose their own horse then go riding.

More often though, the horse came over to you as they loved the companionship, you didn't need a saddle either.

There were lovely woods to ride through, full of wild flowers and scented trees.
There were many lakes to explore, where you could not only ride around the paths, but also swim through

the water with the horses.

They loved swimming around in the lakes along with dolphins and other strange water creatures. The horses loved being there and enjoyed the special relationship with those who rode them. They understood each other's thoughts and exchanged experiences.
Bob rode one horse who had been John's special companion whilst on earth.
The horse showed Bob the journey that they used to take every few weeks.

It began in a city, where his own stable yard was near many small houses crowded together. They called them back to backs, as one was joined onto the back of another. There were usually other horses there with him in the stable yard in their own stalls, who were due to be sold on at the marketplace.

It was interesting that the horse could share his experiences with the other horses in the yard telepathically, and how enjoyable this was for him, especially when there were new ones every week to *talk* to.

Bob was shown this interaction and he hoped that soon, people would realise that animals were more intelligent than was thought and that they had feelings.

When the other horses had been sold, John and

several other men on horseback would meet up on the edge of the city, where they would all ride out together, through the countryside and into the next town.
They always went to the same Inn, and John would spend the evening with his other friends drinking and singing loudly.
The horses were stabled up, where they got a chance to eat hay, drink water, and rest for the night.
That was after the singing stopped of course.

Early the following day they would be brushed down, saddled up and continue on again.
It was a long day but they arrived at their destination which was in Wales. Here they could rest for two days at a lovely farm set in the hills.
This was a stud farm where they bred many horses, it was lovely to see the young foals.

Afterwards, they would make the same journey back to their town, only this time they were joined by several other young horses who were going back to the city to be sold.
The marketplace where the horses were haggled over and then sold on, was a lively, noisy place. The horses would be trotted up and down the street so that the buyer could check that the horse was in good condition.

Bob could follow this journey that the horse was showing him and could feel how strong he was, how he lived in the moment, only focusing on what was happening in the present, it was fascinating.

The horse showed Bob another journey that he and John did occasionally whilst on earth.
It was to a horse fair that was a few miles away in the next town. There would be quite a procession of people and horses all travelling along the road to this popular fair.

There were many other horses there, ready to be bought or sold for a good price. Plenty of other entertainment was laid on, and the pubs were busy all day and night.

It was very crowded and noisy but vibrant. John always went with his best mate and they had a great time meeting up with old friends. They rode back to the town late at night singing and in very high spirits.

One time John and his friend decided to race each other down the high street when they were near home, so both horses galloped flat out down the mainly empty street. Two policemen ran and caught up with them at the end of the street, and were not happy with John and his friend.
The horse told Bob that John had been annoyed for ages after that. 'He always talked to me, but I had to listen to his moaning every day for I don't know how long.'

Bob laughed, he was amused by this little piece of history, he asked John about it when he got back. ' Oh yes I remember, I had to attend court with my friend

and we were each given a large fine though we were only doing *twelve* miles an hour, and down an empty street.
I felt angry for a long time after that,' John laughed.

'What a great life you seemed to have, Bob said, I almost wish that I could have been with you.'
'Yes I enjoyed it though it was hard work, but it kept my family housed and fed. I had ten kids altogether though two died young. But what I liked most about that life was the closeness of friends and neighbours and how we all stuck together and helped each other in time of need.'

Bob was still discovering his own personal journey, there was so much information, so many experiences, covering many lifetimes.

One life was in Africa, in a tribal community, where they had to go out hunting for food in order to survive. It was a physically demanding life, but they were very close, eating and dancing together every night.
He and the others though, were very territorial and had often fought off neighbouring tribes.

He had lived another life in Africa, this time as a female.
Her name was Adisa, and she had married a cold hearted businessman from Portugal who traded in slaves, shipping them from Senegal to Britain.

Adisa had very little empathy herself, she kept the house and staff in order.

She liked to make effigies that looked like tiny dolls, and if anyone annoyed her, she would stick pins into one, hoping that person would become sick.

Later on, her husband felt that he was losing his power and ordered a sacrifice to be made.
It was thought that if a child was sacrificed, the child's energy would be transferred to the leader, giving him more strength.
Unfortunately, two children were sacrificed, but they were her own children. Adisa was furiously determined to have revenge on all those involved.

She had little power to organise anything herself, because for one thing the practice of sacrifice was not unusual at that time. But also she had no rights at all, she was just the property of her husband.
So she used the effigies and made one to resemble every man that had been involved in the sacrifices, and then used all the power that she could muster to hopefully torture and kill them.

She stuck burning hot pins into them day and night, and did appear to see some results. They became ill with a fever and one died, she was so happy that she danced on his grave.

Bob saw that lifetime filled with hatred, because there was no love, no empathy, everything and everybody was viewed as property belonging to someone.
He had been relieved to exit that life shortly after the children died.
During his most recent life in England, he realised

why he hated Africa and had refused to go there, even for a holiday. But also discovered that he had picked up his love of dancing from these two African lives.

The life following the African one was interesting. He had decided to have control of his own life experience, not to be attached to anybody, to feel freedom.
A few souls were going to join him at times to help him get by. But otherwise his life would be to go with the flow.

He was born in seventeenth century Paris as a female, named Reine. As a child she was neglected by her mother and was raised by her grandparents.
They both died when she was thirteen, and suddenly she was on her own, living on the narrow streets in Paris.

She found friends who were also homeless, and they looked after her by letting her shelter with them in an abandoned building.
A shopkeeper also took pity on her and gave her food every day. This was one of the souls who had agreed to help her in this French life.

After a few years she met a woman who offered her a job.
Reine liked this woman from the start and they got on well together, so she took the job.
She needed money anyway now just to survive, and so became a prostitute.
The woman who had hired her, ran a brothel near the river and managed the many clients that came along.

She matched them up with the girls and soon Reine had a group of men to work with. She became their favourite and they formed a sort of friendship with her.
She actually quite enjoyed this lifestyle, having enough money to buy food and clothing and a room that she could afford to rent.
She lived like this until she was thirty one, when she contracted tuberculosis and died a few months later.

Bob looked at that life and though he felt the hardship and sometimes fear, he had really enjoyed the freedom and comradeship.
That French life had also had some impact on his recent English life. He had felt an affinity for Paris whilst taking a holiday there.
He couldn't explain it, but it had felt like a pair of old comfortable slippers, even though the narrow streets had gone.

Most of his other lives were not as colourful as these, but did involve relationships of various sorts. It seemed that relationships with others were important, for the valuable experience you could gain from them.

Bob and all the others were very grateful for the opportunities they had been given to live a life on earth.
They knew that the body was simply the tool for the soul to experience something.
It is your state of being that matters. Are you mainly

angry, uncaring, inconsiderate, distant, resentful etc. Or are you cheerful, friendly, caring and helpful. Your *emotional* state [energy in motion] determines what you attract into your life on earth.

Bob was certainly enjoying himself now though.

He was on his way to meet some friends, walking across a meadow on his way to a nearby wood, when he saw Cornelius sitting on the grass surrounded by a group of souls.

They greeted Bob, and Cornelius explained that he was going to give a talk about bereavement, because most of those who were there, were suffering some long term effects after losing somebody.

Bob then noticed that many of them were still living on earth, their bodies were asleep and now their mind was free to travel. He also saw that each person had someone from the spirit world, sitting next to them.
He realised that the departed one was keeping the person company, hoping they would feel better when they woke up on earth.

That's really nice he thought, he was well aware of how awful it felt to lose someone, especially when you had no idea what may have happened to them.
During his most recent life, Bob had been bought up mainly by his grandparents when his parents had divorced. His father had left home never to be seen again, and his mother was depressed for a long time afterwards.

His grandfather had introduced him to motorcycling as he had one himself.
He often took Bob out on his bike, where they would ride around the country lanes, then stop at a pub and his grandad would buy him a packet of crisps and a glass of lemonade.

He also loved his grandma who was so cheerful.
She cooked all of his favourite foods and made cakes and bread, he even went on holiday with them to their rather small caravan.
But oh, how lovely to swim in the sea and then lie in the warm golden sand.
He remembered this time with happiness.

When they both died within a few months of each other, he was very upset and missed them awfully.

Luckily he had got his wife by then as they were not long married.

Even losing a pet was sad, he had a hamster called Sooty for his eighth birthday and had spent ages making him a nest using newspapers.
He remembered how empty the house had felt when Sooty died.
So he decided to stop and listen to Cornelius for a while.

CHAPTER EIGHT

Bereavement

'Losing someone you love is usually a very painful experience and can put you into great depths of despair. You feel powerless as there is nothing you can do to bring them back, said Cornelius.
Sometimes feeling guilty and reproachful, thinking, 'If only I had done this or that or, if only I had been with you at the moment that you died.

It is also not unusual to feel anger that he left you, and you may think, if only he had tried harder to beat that disease, or if only he had driven the car more carefully.

At first it is painful adjusting your daily routine and future life knowing that the person you loved is not going to be part of it.
So at first, allow yourself to grieve, be kind to yourself, try stress relieving treatments such as a body massage, spa, relaxing in a hot tub or just sleep.

After a few weeks, those awful feelings of despair and powerlessness should have begun to diminish especially as each process of finalising that person's life is completed. The funeral arrangements, then the funeral itself, then clearing out all their personal belongings and finally sorting the finances out.

Most of us adjust, yes feel sad at the loss, but we go back to work or fill the void that has been left. Feeling depressed long after losing someone you loved though, is not a good position to be in.
Your health may be affected and others close to you will feel the effects of your mood.

If you are still feeling depressed and finding it difficult to cope with life, months after their death, try to pinpoint exactly what the difficulty is, do you feel guilty, or angry or maybe you think they have met the ultimate punishment in dying.

Try to see death as being totally normal, the same as being born.
We all die, every living thing is only here for a certain amount of time, and that is not random or a mistake.

You are NOT your body, you are IN your body and it is the most wonderful experience to be released from that dense physical body.

The time we decide to leave is a very individual decision set by our higher mind or soul. It can depend on our current circumstances, but usually pre determined before we were born.

But I don't think anything is set in stone, we are constantly reviewing our life when we sleep when our ego is offline.

One reason for feeling depressed long after you should have moved on with your life, is guilt. Maybe you weren't there at the moment of death and you feel awful, thinking that your loved one died alone.
Surprisingly, this is very common, the family leaves for a short time and whilst you are away the person passes away, as if waiting for you all to leave.

When you think about it, it does make perfect sense. Your life here is finished, you are about to return to the non physical world.
Friends from the spirit world come to meet you to take you there.
But sometimes they find your family gathered around your bed willing you to live.
Their energy can be a hindrance and so it is easier for this process to happen when either no one else is around, or those who are with you, have come to terms with the fact that there is nothing more to do and they just want to be with you.

If your family is desperately trying to keep you here as long as possible, their energy is very real, those intense emotions surrounding you are rather the opposite of what happens when you step out of your body and feel the love and happiness of those who have come to collect you.

Another thing we frequently say when someone dies unexpectedly, is,
' He was in the wrong place at the wrong time.'

We all have to leave our bodies and there are thousands of ways to do this. Maybe when our soul feels it is ready to withdraw from this reality, it guides us to a point in time where for instance an earthquake will occur or a car will spin out of control etc. Perhaps it would be accurate to say ' He was in the right place at the right time' instead.

Again it is our perception of death being an awful punishment, a terrible thing to happen, instead of, our soul is forever but it just decided to spend a short amount of time in physical form to experience something.

When someone dies in a violent and sudden way, it tends to cause the most anguish in those left behind. But many do not want to suffer a long drawn out illness or even a gradual decline in health, going quickly appeals to many people.

When our life is in great danger, we have the ability to withdraw from the body and view the events happening to us as though we were watching another person.

So for instance, if you are falling off a cliff you

will feel the great danger, pull out of your body and observe yourself falling and still screaming because the nervous system still functions and continues to react, but you are outside looking on.

This is true for victims of violent crime too and drowning, any event where our life is put at serious risk. Some people who have had a cardiac arrest and have been revived remember watching the whole event from above their body.
If you are having a hard time because someone you loved died in this manner, it is very likely that they didn't suffer as much as you think.

The solution to getting over a bereavement as quickly as possible is,
At first, give yourself time to get over the shock, soothe yourself as best as you can. It will be a very emotional time until the funeral is over and their personal possessions are sorted.

Focus on the happy times you had together and surround yourself with reminders of those good times. Replay over and over in your mind the events that made you feel happy.

Talk often about your life together, either with others or just to yourself.
The chances are that the departed one is with you anyway, you just can't see them.
Rather than think that you have been permanently separated, try instead to imagine they have just gone on a long holiday.

It is also worth taking into account that out of the two of you, it is only you who is experiencing the pain of separation and that is because of the way they made you feel when you were together.

After dying, those emotions of fear and grief do not exist, all negative emotions are discarded and we only feel loved.
If your belief is that we cease to exist after death, it is still only you feeling the pain of separation.

The best gift you can give to your departed friend is to move on and adjust, try to focus on things that make you happy. Live for today and stop worrying about the past or the future.'

Cornelius carried on with a talk about forgiveness as he thought it followed on nicely. Quite a lot of the others were looking a lot happier already.

FORGIVENESS

We sometimes look to others to provide those things that our parents could not give us, or indeed we may turn into our parents and act in the same way they did. Look at your present relationships and write how you interact with each person in your life.
Is it in a loving balanced way, or are you controlling or too dependent on others, or unable to turn down any request from others, constantly in the giver position.

If a parent was controlling or demanding or needy, you may have become an accommodator. You have little regard for your own needs and are driven to care for others.
If so, are you afraid of being vulnerable and letting go of control, afraid of being loved by others.

There must be a balance in your life of giving and receiving love. It gives us a sense of purpose and makes us feel useful to give of ourselves.
But if you don't accept it from others, maybe you feel that you don't deserve to be loved, then you are saying 'I don't want your love'

Unfortunately, you cannot change another person in the hope that you will feel better, you must change your reaction or attitude to their behaviour.
You cannot walk in another man's shoes, you don't know why they act as they do, why they are driven to negative or destructive acts and often nor do they.
So don't feel guilty and blame yourself for what has happened in the past, but also don't blame someone else for how you are feeling now.

By holding on to resentment, you are still letting that person abuse you, you are letting them live inside your head.
Sometimes though, you feel that the anger is all you have left and you may feel afraid to tolerate the void associated with letting go.

But what you are really doing by letting go of those negative emotions, is releasing all that is not love so that you can create more love in your life.

To forgive someone means to cancel the debt you feel they owe you. It is a surrender and release of the hurt that has passed between you.
It releases the anger and the fear you have been holding on to, allowing you to feel more at peace, more in harmony, more in tune with your inner self.

Make sure you have made a list of everybody who you have been associated with and ask yourself if you are carrying any resentment toward any one on your list.
Write exactly why you resent this person and then

ask, what good can come from this situation. What have I learned from this experience?

Ask, if there is anything you have been unwilling to accept about this. Finally ask what you can let go of for completion, then just write whatever comes into your mind.

If you are feeling guilty or resentful for something you did in the past, or for letting something happen, you must also forgive yourself so that you can move on.

Do this exercise.

Close your eyes and imagine this, it could be now or in the future.
You have died and gone back to being non physical. You are with the friends that you have known before, you all love and support each other and are very close. Also with you, is your spiritual guide who is your mentor and close friend, you are discussing the life you have just left.

What have you done in life that you were pleased with or proud of?
Focus on kindness, bravery, generosity, being a friend etc, and less on the money you have made, your occupation or the holidays you've had.
Why did you react to some event the way you did, could you have changed anything, did you follow your dreams or life plan.

Think about an event you did not like and what solutions were possible.

Try to analyse your past life as though you are making a documentary, how would you evaluate it?
You remember that nothing was set up in your life without your consent, you agreed to be with the parents you had and you planned the major events in your life, to happen the way that they did.

You wanted it to be as real as possible so that you could gauge how you react to a certain situation, and what you could learn from it.

For example, maybe you wanted to learn patience, or perhaps wanted to understand others who are suffering emotional pain, so you chose to live with an alcoholic parent.
Or wanted to experience courage and determination, so you decided to live part of your life with a disability.

Don't feel any guilt (you can't anyway now you've virtually died) just evaluate your life as though you are looking back on it, as though it was a play on stage.

This is a great exercise to do because you are removing yourself from the situation that you are in now and evaluating your life from a different viewpoint
It also doesn't really matter if you don't want to change anything because you cannot get it wrong, but you can be disappointed and feel that your life was wasted if you haven't followed your life plan.

We are all learning how to manage our emotions

and attitudes to situations in life and we cannot be expected to become enlightened, all knowing wise old souls straight away.

Part of being human is to struggle with moral and ethical challenges.
Try to see it as a learning experience, but if you can make anything right, it takes courage but do it, for yourself.
Take no notice of any embarrassment or shame, just free yourself and say sorry or make amends, everyone makes mistakes.

You should only forgive someone if it is safe to do so. It is a different matter if you are in an abusive relationship, forgiving someone every time they hit you is like giving them permission to do it again.

To allow them to be abusive is also not helping them. They are acting from a place of fear when you look at the bottom line.
Their view of reality is different to yours and emotionally, they are not happy.

You need to remove yourself from the situation, then work on your self esteem. Why do you feel the need to be controlled or punished, do you love yourself.
Do the exercises as suggested and then set appropriate and secure personal boundaries that you will not let anyone cross.

APPRECIATION

To deliberately appreciate the simple things in your life on a daily basis, is one of the most powerful things you can do to lift your mood.
Gratitude shifts our perception from what we don't have, to what we do have.
It affirms 'good things are always coming to me.' It instructs your inner mind to respond to you in a positive way.
Whereas anxiety says 'life is terrifying and dangerous, better be careful, don't get your hopes up'

Develop an attitude of gratitude, count your blessings, all of them even the things that seem trivial, say thank you often for all the things that make your life easier.

The more you practise gratitude, the deeper you will be able to feel it and more things to be grateful for will come into your life.
Accept what cannot be changed, happy people don't waste energy on circumstances beyond their control.

Try not to find fault or criticise or complain too often.

They are all negative emotions that lower your mood and unfortunately when you feel depressed, you tend to focus on what's wrong with something, rather than what is positive about it.
Maybe you look for the faults in others rather than their good characteristics.

Some people love to moan about everything and life is a drudge to them, thoughts have been out of control. Inwardly they are saying 'I will never have what I want, no matter how hard I try, it's hopeless, I should just give up'.

As you focus on negative or sad events, other thoughts on the same subject join them. This is because thoughts are magnetic, as you discuss one subject, other similar thoughts on the same subject pop into your mind.

One of the best ways to change negative thoughts and see the world in a better, more light hearted way, is to appreciate or be thankful.
Give up worrying about what you don't have, and focus instead on what you do have and you will find more good things come into your life to be appreciated such as more love, more abundance, more clarity etc.

Try taking a deep breath in then breathe out and hold your breath for as long as possible, then as you take a deep breath in, notice how good that feels. You are breathing in life and as you do, make a wish that your life will be better from now on and you will feel happier.

Take time to tell your family and friends that you are happy they are in your life. Hug your children often and praise them.
Write down anything that you can think of that you like, it could be your favourite food, flower, holiday, friend, sport, shoes etc.

Then go into great detail with each one, what you like about it.
So for instance ' I love my cat, I love the feel of his soft fur and the way I can warm my hands in his fur when they are cold.
I love his cute pink triangle nose and the adorable way he curls up on my lap.'

You get the picture, keep going on your subject, add as much detail as you can using all of your senses.
Do this for all the things you like, maybe adding a few more every day, then as soon as your mood begins to fall lower on the emotional scale, read what you have written.

As part of your daily routine and importantly, as soon as you awake, find things to appreciate or feel grateful for. You can start with your nice soft bed, warm and cosy and relaxing, feel the warm soft covers next to your skin.

As you run the water to have a wash, be grateful for all the workers who over the years have worked hard to

make that possible.
Developing reservoirs to hold the water, clearing debris and parasites so that it is safe to wash in and drink, putting hundreds of miles of pipes underground to get it to your house and then treating all the dirty water so that we don't walk around in sewage when we step outside.

Then there is all the food you eat and the incredible journey and manpower that is needed before it even gets to the supermarket.

You can find many things to be grateful for throughout the day and when you start to do this in a deliberate way, it will change your mood, so simple yet so powerful.
Yes at first you may find that you are just saying the words, but keep it up and soon you will feel the gratitude in your heart and this will start to change your life, it is all about the feelings you are putting out.

It's also not about trying to force yourself to be happy, happiness comes from within so when you decide to focus your attitude on something positive, your inner self will respond, your life will change in the most wonderful way.

It is important to make this part of your daily routine even in circumstances that cause strong negative emotions, like paying bills when you can ill afford to pay them.
As soon as you face a challenge, get busy finding

a solution, don't let the setbacks affect your mood, instead see each new obstacle you face as an opportunity to make a positive change.
Learn to trust your gut instincts, it's almost always right.

Firstly, work out the best solution with the available choices. For instance, can you pay a bill in full, or could you phone the company and agree to pay a certain amount each month, could you see an agency who will help with debt problems.
You are being proactive and positive, there is a sense of freedom in the opportunity to make choices, the effect is motivating. It will stop you panicking and feeling extreme anxiety once a solution has been found.

Next, feel appreciation for the company who has supplied you with the electricity or gas or water or whatever it is that you cannot pay. How it has made your life easier, how you love having it in your home so that you just flick a switch and the room is lit up, or turn on the tap and you get lovely clean hot or cold water.

Be thankful and remember that your own ancestors had to use candles at night and spend hours cleaning out coal fires and how the dust and smog ruined their health and cut their lives short. How their water was usually contaminated with human or animal sewage
Just say to yourself, thank you, as you send off the bill.

You have to be consistent in your practised thoughts, the more you do this, the easier it gets, the better your life becomes.

Before you fall asleep, focus your thoughts on something positive, a holiday you would like, a new career, a loving relationship.

Imagine you have got it, what does it feel like?

When you wake up, appreciate whatever you can as you are getting ready, say to yourself 'I am going to have a great day.'

Try to laugh, don't take yourself or life too seriously, you can find humour in many situations throughout the day.

Laugh at yourself, no one is perfect, being able to laugh at ourselves reflects both self acceptance and humility and keeps the ego in proper perspective.

It is cleansing, if you have ever experienced laughing until your eyes were watering, you can feel the tension being washed away.

Don't get overly concerned with what other people are doing or saying

and try not to judge, everyone has a right to their own life, to live it how they want, including you.

Find the positive side in any situation, know that everything happens for a reason, even though you may not know what that reason is, if a negative thought creeps in, replace it with a positive thought.

Don't take on the world's worries because planet earth at this point in time, is being perfectly normal.

What if right now, there was no corruption, wars or

conflict of any sort and everything was perfect. We would be unable to evolve any further, to learn from mistakes or wrong choices that we made.

We would be unable to experience being unloved, so then appreciate what being loved is truly like and then having the empathy to understand others in the same situation.

We must be able to experience cold in order to know what hot means, we want this contrast in order to grow, to become more than we were before.

See the world as a vast playground for people to experience anything they want. Some will stay on the slow, safe rides this time, whilst others will want the thrill of the roller coasters for the exhilarating experience.

This is exactly how you came into this life, throwing in a few challenges.
Most of us would not have wanted a perfectly safe, boring life where nothing much happens and I am referring to our higher mind or soul, not our ego.

We want to be stretched a bit and experience different roles. Adversity
provides an opportunity for us to grow and mature in ways that would be difficult living an easy life.
Those you hate are often our greatest teachers, yes our fragile ego takes a knock and unfortunately we often

keep regurgitating those hurtful feelings for years after the event, but try to find the deeper wisdom that you may have gained.

Our soul will draw us to the experience we want, even though our ego mind can't see it. Loosen your grip on things, let go, lighten up, resistance does not feel good. It's all about smelling the roses as they say and looking for things to appreciate all through the day.
As you direct your attention to looking for things that please you, your whole outlook on life will change because thoughts are magnetic and more nice things to appreciate will come into your life.

If you are worrying about the future or feeling resentment for the past, then these thoughts are what you will get more of and they are counterproductive to feeling happy. You are spoiling what should be a happy, joyful life.
Stop focusing on what you do NOT want, and focus on what you do want.
It doesn't really take much effort.

Do you love yourself ? The answer should be yes. If you answered no or are not sure, it's time to change your attitude. When you feel comfortable and confident in yourself, it is much easier to connect and feel affection for others.

You are much more than a physical body, though it is a magnificent machine for us to experience everything in life, you are so much more than that.
It is important to remember that you are not your

body, you are in your body, a big difference.
We are each unique, there is no one else anywhere that has shared exactly the same experiences, we are being perfectly normal for our development at this time.

Don't wait until the end of your life and look back with regret that you could have been happier if only.
Be true to yourself, not put on a front of how others want you to be. Live your dreams, write about how you want your life to be.
Have respect for yourself because you are unique and don't put up with being someone else's emotional baggage.

Learn to express your feelings in a loving way, as others will respond more positively than when being yelled at. It is never good to suppress your feelings in order to keep the peace with others.
If you carry bitterness and resentment, it will be like poison preventing you from being happy and may also cause chronic illness. Let this go, transform it.

Be like a child sometimes, be silly, have fun and laugh. Life isn't meant to be serious all the time. Stop being afraid of what others think about you, make the most of your life and be happy.

Close friends are important in your life because they have often shared many other lives with you. Sometimes you can sense this when you first meet someone and there is an instant attraction.
As though they went on holiday and now you are just picking up where you last left off. You feel comfortable

with that person from the moment you meet.
Do make time to keep in touch with friends, because when you hit a rocky patch in your life, you may need them.

Bob loved this, he knew that humans were often very serious about life. He thought that life could be better if they laughed more, or just observed how children enjoy the simplest things.
Yes, thought Bob, it is fun walking through a pile of red and gold autumn leaves, or jumping in puddles.

Bob remembered that when he went into the town, there would often be a busker or small band playing some nice music.
He always felt like dancing along to the catchy songs, but never did.
He thought he would look stupid being the only one dancing, but now he wished that he hadn't cared what others thought.
He would have had fun and some may even have joined in.

He left the group and carried on to a small wood, where his friends were doing some work.
A group of children had asked them to design a treehouse for them to play in. They had been around Bob's dirt track with their go karts and were impressed with the cool things that were always being added to make it interesting, they knew that Bob and his friends would make them a great tree house.

They weren't wrong either, the design had been completed and there was not one, but five tree houses. Each small wooden house was in a different tree, all of various heights. They were all connected with ramps or ropes and bridges, so that they could easily walk from one to the other.
Bob and the others then added the *extras.*

A couple of water sprinklers were put up in the trees, so that the children had to run from the bridge through the water, they would have great fun doing that.
They added some of the golden balls that were full of glitter, though now, they had to be hit with a stick and the glitter would fly out and cover them.
Bob had to tone down the glitter though, otherwise the children would sparkle like xmas trees.

They designed and made some toys, though these were far better than any that Bob remembered. There were six small black monkeys that could jump through the trees and swing on the branches. They were so cute.

Bob designed some brightly coloured parrots that could sing and talk and even dance with the children, he knew they would love these.
Alex built a tiny fort in the highest tree, it looked like the one he had haunted for many years, so the design didn't need much thought.
He then made four yellow birds with large red wings, so that the children could sit on them and fly around,

or get a ride up to the fort.

They put in a helter skelter from one of the tree houses, it was very long and went spiralling to the ground, they all had a go on it and declared it great fun.
Bob fixed a row of swings onto a tree, then when the children sat on them and shouted 'GO' they would all swing around together, until they shouted STOP.

It really was similar to a theme park. Bob wanted to put in a boat ride, but the others thought that was going a bit too far, especially when they had only been asked to make one treehouse.

When the children saw their treehouse park, as they called it, they were so thrilled, they thanked Bob and his friends, and all ran off to play.
Alex said it had been so much fun making the tree house park and the others agreed.

Bob had joined a band with Alex and some other friends, now that he had mastered playing the guitar.
The music was a bit odd because Alex played the bagpipes and Ron was the drummer, making the music a very odd mix.
But all together they were not too bad, and others came to listen and dance along to their novel sounds, the music worked and the tunes were very catchy.

They all loved playing and found they had a talent for inventing new songs that would fit in with their instruments. Alex had to speed up his bagpipes so that

the sound fitted in with the drums.
They chose to play in a circular enclosed space, so that you felt as though you were on the bottom of the lake. The backdrop was like an aquarium with octopus and fish swimming around you, it was quite fascinating. Even Isabella and her friends came and danced along to the music.

Bob still loved to travel around different planets and galaxies, he was fascinated by the multitude of life forms all in various stages of development. There were some that were more advanced spiritually than those on earth and Bob had found one race particularly interesting.

This was because the people on this planet could actually see him and talk to him telepathically. They looked slightly similar to humans as they had two legs and arms. But their heads were larger, they had no hair, small mouths,and very big eyes.

He discovered they had once been similar to humans in their development, but had become more spiritually advanced over time. They were about two thousand years ahead of humans

They took time every day to deliberately appreciate things around them, because as they said, if you find things to appreciate, the universe sends more things to you to appreciate.
It is the law of attraction, and they certainly

incorporated it into their lives.

They also told him that they followed their highest excitement. Every time there were choices to be made, the one that gave them the best feeling would be chosen, again this was them asking the universe to send more things to be excited about.
But it also allowed them to live in the moment, they did not make plans for the future. They had what they wanted, at the time they wanted it.

One of the things they loved doing was teaching others, not on their own planet but those who were not as spiritually advanced as them.
When the inhabitants of a planet were ready, usually when they were on the verge of space travel, they would begin to make contact with them.
They did this in a similar way to Bob, when he had joined his energy with the bee..

These beings would have permission to join up with someone, often called channelling. It was a collaboration between them both. Then they could use the vocal cords to communicate and others could then ask questions.

The discussions were mainly about how to be happy with life, the best way to solve problems, the importance of knowing yourself, what was out there in the universe etc.

The next stage was to make physical contact with the people where they could offer more practical help.
Bob was told that this would happen within the next few years on earth.

They had spacecraft and could travel to far distant regions of the galaxy.
To them though, travelling was not how *we* do it, moving physically from A to B.

They had learnt that you could set up a vibrational frequency of where you want to be, then transport there instantly.
Bob learnt that they often came to earth because it was going through some significant changes right now.

On earth, the old system was crumbling away which was causing a lot of upheaval. But it was bringing in a new era, where earth would be a better place to live.

They and other interested beings were closely watching this great change in humanity, there was much to learn from it.

There had also been much discussion on whether we would end up destroying the planet.
They saw what little regard we had for it, how we couldn't see that it was a living thing. The trees were the lungs of the earth and these were being chopped down at an alarming rate.

The rivers and seas were polluted, these are the

arteries and veins of the planet, and the amount of chemicals and pesticides used was alarming, poisoning not only the planet but also the wildlife and us humans.

Bob mentioned that the people were trying to reduce global warming, but he was told that this would have happened anyway, it was normal for the earth to have periods of warming and cooling.

There had after all been a mini ice age less than three hundred years ago, but now, humans are accelerating the warming of the planet, though it would happen anyway, but to a lesser degree.

Some aliens also have a close interest in us because we are related to them from thousands of years ago. We share some of their DNA and they consider us as family.

He loved how these aliens now lived in harmony and hoped those on earth would follow their path.
He saw that the present situation on earth might be a wake up call.

CHAPTER NINE

Bob was following the events happening on earth very closely, because he was thinking about coming back to experience life as a human.
He worked out that his last incarnation was about thirty five years ago in earth time, and he was now feeling the need to move on.
He had been to see the three elders again, the same souls that he met at his life review and they had discussed all of the options together.

The first choice was to follow a more or less similar life to his last one, where he would be a family man, living in a suburban town in a western society.
The elders though were not so keen on this choice, they thought that a different approach was needed.

The next choice was similar, but he would be single and instead of a family, he would be a manager of a large company.
It would mean that he would have less control over people's personal lives, but would have to manage a large workforce who would be like a family substitute

for him.
The trouble was, he may then expect too much from his employees and create a lot of friction.

His final choice was that he lived with a small group of people in a remote area.
He would not be able to control anything here as they would all work together, they would discuss anything important and would all vote on the outcome.

Of course there would be the odd test, where he could judge how he would react.

'Do you know Joshua,' asked one.
'Oh yes said Bob, he often visits us.'
'Well he is planning an earth life, he wants to be an explorer, learning about remote communities and finding rare animals.
He has agreed to visit your village for a short time, where he will have many interesting tales to tell.
He will be very popular with some of the women especially, and will certainly stir things up.

As you know, he was in one of your previous lives, in Africa where he was living in a different tribe to yours.
He was one of your rivals and you fought each other once or twice, so when you encounter him again, in this coming life, you may feel some resentment toward him, deep down.

But you may also put that behind you and find that he is very interesting, as he will have travelled far and sailed on the seas all around the globe.

When you listen to his romantic tales of adventures in far away countries, you will have a yearning to follow him, because you also have pleasant soul experiences of travelling.

But in this life, you will not be able to. It will give you the opportunity to feel what it is like to be confined, to lose your freedom to get out and explore.
He will be a catalyst for you to have a very valuable experience.

'What about if I decide to have nothing to do with him?' asked Bob.
'He won't be alone, there are two others with him, they are all from the same soul group, an adventurous lot who are excellent communicators.
Believe me, you will be transfixed with their stories.'

This was the elders' choice for him, they could see that this life would have a nice harmonising, balancing effect, there would be just enough friction as a test. Bob thought this was a great idea, so he went back to his friends to think about what he would like to do.

He decided to go to the library and take a look at his most recent lives. He wanted to feel the emotions again, see how intense they were, and try to work out if he could overcome his tendency to control others in any of the three lives he had been shown.
He examined each life very carefully, and felt the very strong feelings and emotions in those past lives.

Maybe he should go with the elders' recommendation.

Of course he knew that if he did fail this test that he was setting for himself, it wouldn't really matter.
It was common to need several lifetimes in order to learn something, but he didn't want to waste this life and then feel the need to repeat it again.

Also, the rest of his group were doing very well.
They had set goals for themselves and were very happy with their achievements.

Eliza also had a tendency to cling on to people, and she had set herself a test to overcome. She was now experiencing her life on earth.
She was living her life in Australia as a male, and Bob often went to see how she was getting on.
The test was that her partner (wife) would have to leave home for at least a year to take care of her ageing parents who lived in another country.
Eliza could have tried any number of tactics to prevent her from leaving, but didn't.

She hadn't wanted her partner to leave and had wrestled with it in her mind, but had then acted unselfishly and gave her full blessing.
She passed with flying colours, she found a hobby that kept her occupied and spent more time with friends.

Bob was very proud of her and so were the rest of the group. They were all overcoming obstacles and tests they were setting for themselves, so Bob didn't want to be left behind.

There was something else he could do though to help

make a final decision.
He went back to the large dome-like building that Alistair had taken him to.
It was the same place where he had come for his life review, but part of the building was set up as a place where you could review your possible future life before making a decision on whether to go ahead with it.

Bob went inside and was taken to a beautiful room that felt very organic.
The light was a bit subdued which added ambience to the two trees that grew through the room and up through the ceiling.
Right at the front of the room was what looked like a suspended waterfall. Similar to a small screen but not flat, it was a moving shimmering energy.
Bob walked right up to it and watched to see what it would show him.

He saw the highlights of each of the three lives, beginning with the first.
He observed his wife and children in what felt like a normal family life.
Later he witnessed an argument he and his wife were having.
It seemed that now the children were older, she wanted to go on a holiday with her friends.

They were two of her girlfriends that she had known since childhood, and because they were all having a birthday, they thought that it would be nice to go

away together as one owned a villa.
This was reasonable because she and Bob were with each other most of the time and did nearly everything else together.

At this point Bob could actually stand inside the screen and feel the emotion he was having at that time in this life.
He began to feel a bit of panic as he was arguing, an old familiar feeling from his last life.
Maybe not as strong but it felt as though she was abandoning him.
He knew that nobody else had caused this, it was totally him and his fears.
He stood watching and tried to work out if he would be able to overcome this fear when he was living the real life on earth.

The second life was rather similar but in a different way. He could see that his employees were like a family to him, because they were all he had in his life.
He stepped into that life and felt the pleasure of owning this big company and all the people working for him.

But he also began to feel a need to keep them in his life where he felt happy, and this was at work. Unfortunately this would clash with their lifestyle, where they had families to go home to.
He had to decide whether he could develop outside interests, or would he be focused solely on his business.

The final life was set in a beautiful place where he saw the friendly group of people who lived there.
They were very close, they worked together and raised the children together, all one big family. Bob saw Joshua enter his village and stepped into the screen to experience the emotions.

He did immediately feel some conflict with having a stranger there, but the emotion was more subdued than how he had felt with the other two lives.
Perhaps that was partially because all the others were very excited. It was rare to see other people in their village, and Joshua and his two friends had bought a few gifts for them.

Bob had to decide which life would be best for him. On the plus side he was not going to create any trauma in his childhood, which he hoped would not cause the same negative feelings later as an adult.
But also, his memories would be removed so that the experience could be totally authentic, so he would have to go with his gut and his ego.
It was not an easy choice for Bob.

Although he knew that the choice would be down to him, he wanted to discuss it with his friends. So he met up with Ron, George, Alex and Isabella who were sitting on their sailing boat discussing their future plans together.
Bob told them of his choices and how he was having difficulty deciding what to do.
He asked the others what their plans were.

'I'm planning an earth life right now' said Isabella. 'I will be part of a team where we will build bases for people to live, usually in difficult places.
These will be self-contained small towns that don't rely on the outside atmosphere.
So perhaps they will be built under the sea on the ocean bed, or even in a base on the moon where people can live or just go for a holiday.'

'Wow, how exciting,' said Bob, ' I'll probably be stuck in a jungle in this next life, but will certainly visit in the following one. Of course it makes sense since you love designing buildings and towns.
How about you Alex.'

' I'm going with her because I am good at organising groups of people. Though there won't be any major conflicts, there will be plenty of work to keep me interested.
We are going to be man and wife and work together, it will be great.

Our life will be a link between our people on earth and other aliens from different planets, because by then we will hopefully have contact with them.
We will also be learning some building techniques from them.'

The others thought that this life suited them both perfectly.
'So long as you don't build a pizza hut on the moon.'
They laughed.

The others thought that Bob should experience the *jungle life,* as he called it.
'It's not too dissimilar from our self contained towns' said Alex.
'A group of people living together in a remote area. Just build a dirt track, then you will be happy.'

'If Bob decides to go for this life, then I'm going to join him, ' said Ron.
I've always had an interest in herbs and rare plants, and this life will give me a great opportunity to explore the dense jungle and study them.

When the travellers come to visit, I am leaving with them and can share the information that I have discovered with the wider population.'

'Yes, said Bob, it will be nice to have a close friend with me for this life.
We have spent other lives together, usually as brothers and that's what we are planning now. When the traveller's leave, my experience will have come to its conclusion, so I will be back here shortly afterwards.'

He didn't want to live to an old age, but wanted just enough time to have the experience that had been planned.

George wasn't planning anything yet, he was staying there for now. He wished the others luck though and promised to look after the boat.

Bob was going to go and listen to another talk explaining the importance of meditation when on earth, because it always helps by letting you connect to your higher mind.

He could always factor this into his lives, but would he follow it through when he was there.
There would also be a discussion given by Cornelius, on what future earth may look like.

He found a large group already waiting for the talk to begin, so he joined some of his friends as they sat in the meadow. They listened enthralled as Cornelius began.

MEDITATION

'Meditation allows our ego mind to rest and we then become closer to our higher mind where all solutions are, it is a way of regaining contact with ourselves.
We are often afraid to be completely alone with our own thoughts.
The first thing we usually do when coming home to an empty house is turn on the television or put music on. Yes, we are sociable beings and prefer company, but as *you* are the most important person in your life, it is not good to lose contact with yourself.

When you begin to have conversations with yourself and learn to tune in to your emotional state, you will learn to love the relationship you have with yourself and gain insight into how to solve problems and feel comfortable and at peace with your own company.

You will be in control and feel good to be on your own, be your own best friend rather than expecting others to make you feel happy. People come and go throughout your life and are not always dependable, so it is very important to be happy with yourself.

There are different ways to meditate but the most

classic is to sit comfortably in a quiet place, then breathe deeply in and out, slowly, just keeping your attention on your breathing. By focusing on your breathing, your ego, or physical mind eventually becomes bored and takes a nap.

You will know when this has happened because you will then feel relaxed and rather detached and weightless. Your higher mind will always be sending you images or solutions to any problem you may have, but now while meditating, you are in a receiving mode.

The constant chatter of your ego has stopped, and for a while you are in close contact with your higher self. You just get out of your own way for a whilst.

It takes a bit of practice at first because your ego mind is full of chatter and is probably used to being in the control seat and so sends the most random thoughts to distract you.
Just brush the thought to one side and focus on your breathing again.
If you want, you can ask for a solution to a particular problem, before you begin meditating. You will then be in a great receptive state to get a reply.

There are other ways to meditate and also, many types of music made especially for relaxation that you can listen to.
One is walking meditation where you simply walk whilst focusing on a problem.

Go to a local park and find a quiet path, take a few deep breaths and walk for one or two miles while focusing your mind. Or walk up and down a swimming pool or even walk back and forth at home.

Jogging can produce this altered state too and so too I believe, the sport of fishing, I'm sure the most active mind would soon get bored watching a float for hours.

In fact, any repetitive movement will bore the ego mind eventually.

Try to meditate once a day for about 15 minutes if you can.
Relaxing and meditating are the process of letting go.
As you begin to ignore the stimuli from the senses, the ego mind will drift off, just notice breathing in and out. You can also think to yourself the word relax as you exhale.

Meditation is also very beneficial if you are suffering from chronic pain.
It usually diminishes quite considerably, it is well known that feeling stressed or depressed makes pain feel worse.

The further down the mood chart you are, the more you will be affected by any physical problem you have.

You will begin to feel inspired and receive creative insight as you allow your higher mind to flow in harmony.

Prayer does have a place in that you have put out a request, but the ego mind is so full of chatter and distraction that you need to quieten it so that you can listen for the answer.
Or indeed look for the answer to show up in your life.

So prayer and meditation go together.

We also enter a relaxed state every night just before falling asleep.

It is an ideal time to change a characteristic that you don't like about yourself or even to play out your dreams for the future, so now this is a good time to talk about the law of attraction.

LAW OF ATTRACTION

There is a field of energy where your desires are created, in an energy form.
So over your lifetime there will be hundreds of things in there that you have wished for, such as a home, clothes, holidays, health, security, a mate etc.
It is what we all constantly do as it helps us to expand and grow.
We do usually get what we are wishing for eventually, but there is a way to get your desires in a much quicker way.

We have the language to use that field of energy, but it only understands emotion, so this is how you have to ask.

Thought and emotion are one, so create the feeling in your heart as if your wish is already answered. This creates the electrical and magnetic waves that bring it to you.

So for example, if you want a new car imagine that

you have it now.

It is there in front of you. Sit in the driver's seat, smell the leather, put your hands on the steering wheel, turn on the radio and listen to your favourite music. Have a photo of your car and feel excited every time you look at it.

Evoking this feeling is the same for anything that you want.

So if you want a holiday, imagine what it feels like as you walk along the beach with the sand between your toes, and the sun on your back. Imagine a nice cold ice cream in your hand and feel it on your tongue as you walk through a warm sandy rockpool.

Get your suitcase ready and the clothes you want to wear, feel excited that you are going. Don't jeopardise it by thinking that you can't afford it, or some other excuse.

Your ego mind is not meant to work out how you are going to get it, your holiday may happen in an unexpected way.

This works because when you have asked for something, it is created in a reality that could be your future. There are infinite realities and you are making choices all of the time.

From which street to walk down, what soap to buy, where to have lunch and what to eat etc.

So you are creating a future reality and then living in it. Usually you don't think about these choices, they just seem to be automatic.

But there is the art of deliberate creation. So for instance, if you want a nice new red car, you will begin to notice these exact cars showing up in your life. You may notice them on the road or see pictures of the car.

This is to ask, is this what you want, it is a sign that you are getting close to having your desire.

Just don't feel jealous of those who already have what you desire, or you will not manifest it. Because then, you are not creating something, instead you are wishing that someone else goes without.

Feeling envy is different, it is striving for something that you want. You are wishing that you had it.

There is usually a time lag because your inner mind will be making sure that you want this.

You must now live as if you are in that future you want. Feel as though you are there living the dream because words alone are not enough.

You must feel the emotion of having it, at least sixty seconds of concentrated thought will bring more exciting thoughts on the object you desire.

Then take any physical action that feels good, in order to achieve this. Yes you can go down the work hard route, but this is more fun.

Suppose you want money, but trying to manifest it

is not working. Can you truly feel the money in your hand or is there some resistance when you are asking?

This could be because there may be a belief in your subconscious mind that you picked up in your childhood. Such as 'money is the root of all evil or money doesn't grow on trees etc.'
You need to deal with whatever that belief is first. Or better still, concentrate your thoughts on what you would buy with the money when you have it.

It takes practice at first so begin with manifesting something small. Maybe a white feather or a pound coin, a green hair band, or imagine someone bringing you a drink. Feel it in your hand, taste it, imagine you've got it, draw a picture of it and pin it up where you can see it often.

This is deliberately manifesting your desire with the expectation that you will receive it. It only takes practice because we have lost the art of deliberately creating things into our lives and you do need faith that things you have asked for will appear.

Probably less than one percent of the population practice this art of deliberate creation, and they are usually the very successful ones, but more are realising that this is the way forward.

You can also manifest solutions for the planet as a whole, groups of people working together are very powerful.

There may be exceptions where manifestation won't work, for example where you have set an intention to live a life in a certain way and within the rules of the time period. So maybe you plan to live in a body that has different chromosomes, such as Down's syndrome or some other disorder.

You won't be able to change your physical appearance, although lifestyle changes are achievable.

Before falling asleep at night, imagine one thing that you would like in your life right now. Maybe a perfect holiday or being happy, a new car, a loving partner, more money or even just walking around a lovely park if you rarely go out.
Pick one subject and have fun with it, get into the feeling of having it or being there.

Go gradually with things that may have some emotion attached to them.
One of these may be weight loss, set your target for a lower number at first, a few pounds at a time.
Helpful affirmations may be the answer, repeat at least fifty times a day how you see your weight. *I am ten stone, I look better, my clothes fit, I can walk easier.*
Say it until it sounds easy, put photos where you can see them of a time when you were slimmer.
Using all your senses add as much detail as you can.

For a new mate, imagine being together in a place that you love. As you walk along, hold hands and feel close. Laugh together and share a wonderful meal feeling completely at ease with one another.

Find things that you can do together, make it fun, it's your imagination. Make room in your house or life as if he is already there.

Even if you find it difficult to go out and just want to walk around a park, use all of your senses.
Take off your shoes and feel the cool grass on your feet, the lovely warm sun on your back.
Stop at a patch of buttercups shining brightly in the sun and notice the perfect shape of each flower.
Eat a delicious ice cream whilst watching a band playing your favourite music in the park.

Let this be fun and light hearted, use your imagination and focus. Do not bring anything negative into your thoughts.
Doing this will not only replace the worry or sadness that you may feel at this time when you are tired, but it will also help you feel in a better mood when you wake in the morning.
This exercise will also help bring what you are focusing on into your life.

Begin repeating positive words many times throughout the day, these are called affirmations and are statements that allow the experience of what you want.

Repeating an affirmation many times a day keeps you focused on your goal, strengthens your motivation and programs your subconscious to begin to accept what you are asking and do whatever it takes to make that goal happen.

Repeat often to yourself statements like, 'I am confident and strong, I love myself, nothing is more important than that I feel happy, I am lovable, I am successful, I am abundant.'
Or make up your own statements that sound good to you.

Don't start with '*I want*' as in, I want to be happy, as this implies that you want this in the future and don't have it now and you need to be focused on what you want now.

Working with suggestions like these does not mean pounding the thought into your mind in an attempt to drive out other thoughts. It is more an affirmation of truth, said in a casual way as if to imply, no doubt about it.
It works because subconsciously we don't know the difference between what is coming in through our senses, our reality, compared to what we are wanting or pretending will be.

It is vitally important to put the right suggestions into your subconscious mind as it is always acting on the information we are inputting, what we say about ourselves, our emotional state, how we feel on a daily basis.

Saying positive affirmations many times throughout the day will help you begin to believe it and your subconscious mind will begin to overwrite any negative beliefs you have about yourself.

When you value yourself, you become open and friendly, slow to take offence and quick to forgive. People react to you in a more positive way.

If you can't sincerely believe that you can manifest your desire, you can remove the element of personal gain.
You do this, by giving what you are wishing for to another and without expecting anything in return.

This works because the act of giving something away, causes the mind to come to the conclusion that...... *you* must already have *this* or you would not be giving it away.
In other words, you are a prosperous person. Therefore, you have now moved into the reality that you wished for.

If you want to be prosperous, give something to another.
Be loving to others if you want more love in your life.

Imagine that it is your last chance to change these things and these gestures would then be enhanced.

We are always creating anyway, it is in our nature. Whether you are wishing for more food, or a luxury yacht. It is what you feel a need for at that time, but needs always change.

Don't fall into the trap of always thinking, if I have this then I can feel happy. Moving on from one thing to another looking for happiness.
It is important to feel happy first, feeling appreciation for the basic things in your life.

....

There was now going to be a break, so that everyone could discuss what had been said so far.
Bob was sitting with some friends, he had been very impressed.
'I love these talks, they are so enlightening, I do hope they are helping those who are still on earth.'

'Oh yes they have helped my friend here a lot,' said Maggie who was sitting nearby. She was sitting next to her close friend Mabel, who was still living a life on earth.

Bob and the others knew that Maggie had not long died *herself*, because she and Mabel were sitting on the grass with a flask of tea, two cups, and a plate full of chocolate eclairs.

'I hope you are enjoying yourself here Maggie and have settled in ok,' said Bob.
'Oh yes, I absolutely love it, I've met all my old friends. We had so much to catch up on, and I love my cottage and garden, I've even got three of my cats here.

I'll be pleased when Mabel joins me here, but it is not quite her time to come over yet, is it Mabel.' Mabel shook her head and took a sip of tea.

'You see, me and Mabel were lifetime friends, we even bought a retirement flat next to each other.
But I began to get a bit confused and they sent for the doctor.
He came wearing a mask, and tried to explain to me that there were others in the building who had the flu, and because of this, we were not allowed any visitors.

Even my family couldn't visit and I was locked in and couldn't leave.
I felt so angry and screamed at the doctor, he couldn't get through to me so went out to get some help.
Shortly afterwards a huge white dalek strolled into the room. *Well*, I was so scared that I hid under the bedclothes, I screamed the place down and had to be sedated in the end.'

The others were intrigued, 'were you just confused and having visions,' they wanted to know.
'Oh no, I was told afterwards that the person who was coming to help me, was wearing what was called a hazmat suit.
They didn't want to catch the flu, and so had dressed up in this huge white suit from head to toe.'

The others laughed, they imagined how scary that must have been.
'Anyway, she continued, I died a couple of weeks later, but my friend Mabel here has been inconsolable ever since, especially now she is on her own so much.

I am staying with her as much as I can, but her life is depressing at the moment.
Though these outings to listen to Cornelius are good for her.'

The others could just imagine how lonely she was feeling right now, but they all knew that she would shortly be coming over, her life on earth was coming to an end.

Cornelius came back to continue his talk, he had been chatting with some of the others.
He continued,

'This is such a momentous time in earth's history, where at the moment huge changes are happening.

Everything needs to come out into the open to be dealt with, much like agitating the bottom of a fish tank to

release the old dirt and grime.
New discoveries will be found that will help humanity move forward, and soon people will realise that they create their own reality and will take control of their own lives.

It is certainly an interesting time to be part of this change, this is why so many of you are on earth right now, wanting to experience all that is going on.

It has been like pressing a reset button on earth, and humanity has now got a chance to decide on how they would like their future to be.
When all the chaos has settled down it will hopefully look like this.

FUTURE EARTH

1. Know yourself

You become aware of your emotional state throughout the day and take steps to adjust any feelings in order to stay as positive as you can. You will always be aiming for how you want your future to be.

Out of all the choices that you can make every day, you always follow your highest excitement or the choice that feels the best. This will sharpen your intuition and train your mind to bring the best things into your life.

You will immerse yourself in whatever you are passionate about, be driven to succeed. Though if you feel driven to do something that is immoral, you will recognise that anxiety is the feeling behind it all.

2. Meditate

This puts you in tune with your higher mind, letting your instincts guide you, knowing your life's plan

and making better choices. The things that you desire throughout your life, will come to you much more easily.
Meditation will also help you to feel more relaxed and it reduces anxiety.

We will also incorporate this into schools as it also benefits children.
Teaching will change to become more interactive and instead of making children fit into the system, the system will have to fit each child.

We will explore the strengths, desires and gifts of each individual and teaching will be aimed at bringing out the best of these abilities.
Instead of now where we try to cram a bit of everything into every child regardless.

There will be a more practical hands-on approach to teaching, because an experience of physically doing something is likely to be remembered easier than having to retain facts written in a book.

Children will be taught history in a more balanced way, with facts from all involved. They will be encouraged to come to their own conclusions and have a better understanding of how to solve problems.

3. Manifesting your desires

As this becomes better understood, it will become normal to have everything that you desire, including safety and freedom.

There will be no need for the police, military, or control of any sort. One of the best ways to get what you want, is to deliberately appreciate things throughout your day. By doing so, you are always then attracting more things to come into your life to appreciate.

We will all realise that we are constantly shifting into realities creating our future as we move along. Much like jumping from one film strip to the next, billions of times per second.

But as there are many film strips, each telling a different story, we will learn how to jump into the reality we want just by changing the way we think. By imagining and feeling that you are already living in that reality, you will shift into that new timeline.

So by feeling the emotion of having your desire now, will mean joining the reality where it is.

4. As our vibrational energies increase, they will become closer to our soul energy which is on a much higher frequency, and as we become closer to it, we will begin to sense those souls that are in the spirit world.

Eventually we will be able to have conversations with those departed ones. We will all have this ability to tune in and continue to have a relationship with them.

We will also be close to the source energy, or God. Feeling the love in our hearts, simply by asking to be close. It will be a natural state, and have nothing to do with what religion you follow.

5. We will discover the true purpose of our ancient monuments and standing stones. Human bodies have energy points on different areas of the body, we tap into these with acupuncture needles so that the energy can flow freely and help with healing.

Earth is just the same, it is not just a large lump of rock. It is a living thing, it gives us life and sustains us.

On the earth's surface, there are energy points that early humans knew about. They marked these places with standing stones so that others would be able to find them.

The energy in these places is of a higher frequency and has the ability to accelerate healing. Many people came to these special sites in order to be healed.

There would be rituals based on getting into a positive state of mind and people would walk round and round the stones, stirring up the energy to keep it strong.

This energy also raises your vibrational frequency, helping you to become more insightful and sharpening your intuition.
In the future these places will once again be revered and used for their special properties.

Stonehenge is a powerful energy site that thousands of people once travelled to. There are many such places with a higher vibrational energy, such as Ayers rock in Australia, Lourdes in France and many other well known landmarks.
There are many other smaller energy points on earth and these would often be marked with a standing stone or a church would be built on the site. The ancient art of dowsing could easily find them.

Some very ancient sites such as pyramids, contain records of our distant past. Our true origins of how we began our earth lives. That we are indeed part of a galactic family who are waiting for us to be ready to meet them again.

Their DNA was integrated with the indigenous natives living on earth thousands of years ago. Proof will be found and records and artefacts that have been hidden from us by the elite few, will be revealed, finally.

6. Scientists will realise that everything is made of vibrational energy, and that all things have a vibrational signature. A flower has its own unique signature, as does a virus, or water, or insects etc.

They will understand how to copy a particular

signature, then reproduce it in another location, and from that, will be able to teleport objects.

We will also relearn how to levitate objects, it is a skill we once knew thousands of years ago, but has become forgotten over time.

It is how the old pyramids were built, using specific sound frequencies. Each stone would be coated in a substance that melts the outer layer and then it would be levitated into place where it would bind tightly to the next stone.

7. We will eventually be ready to meet aliens from other planets, some of whom share our DNA. We will *all* benefit from their knowledge and will learn so much from them.

This is the way that humanity is heading, just the natural conclusion for humans. There are billions of other cultures all in different states of evolution, all on the one journey back to source energy.

Bob though, was going to be beginning a new life on earth when the time was right. He was excited even though there were big changes happening right now, but it would be a privilege to be part of such a momentous change in humanity.

Bob could see that if humans could transform themselves into the loving beings they were meant to become, they would give hope to many other species living on other planets.

Because others would observe that humans have had to evolve from beginning from a very low vibrational level.

So if it is possible for us to change from being so barbaric, to becoming an enlightened race of people, is a great achievement. If we can do it, they will realise that they can follow our example.

Bob knew that it takes a strong spirit to go into that depth of limitation and forgetfulness and yet still be capable of remembering who you are and bringing light back into your life.

Earth is indeed a master graduating class.

◆ ◆ ◆

In a small village in the Peruvian mountains, a young couple were celebrating.
The other neighbours visited their makeshift house bringing gifts, they were all happy that a baby boy had been born.

His parents had named him Roberto, but he became known as BOB.

Printed in Great Britain
by Amazon

28825795R00128